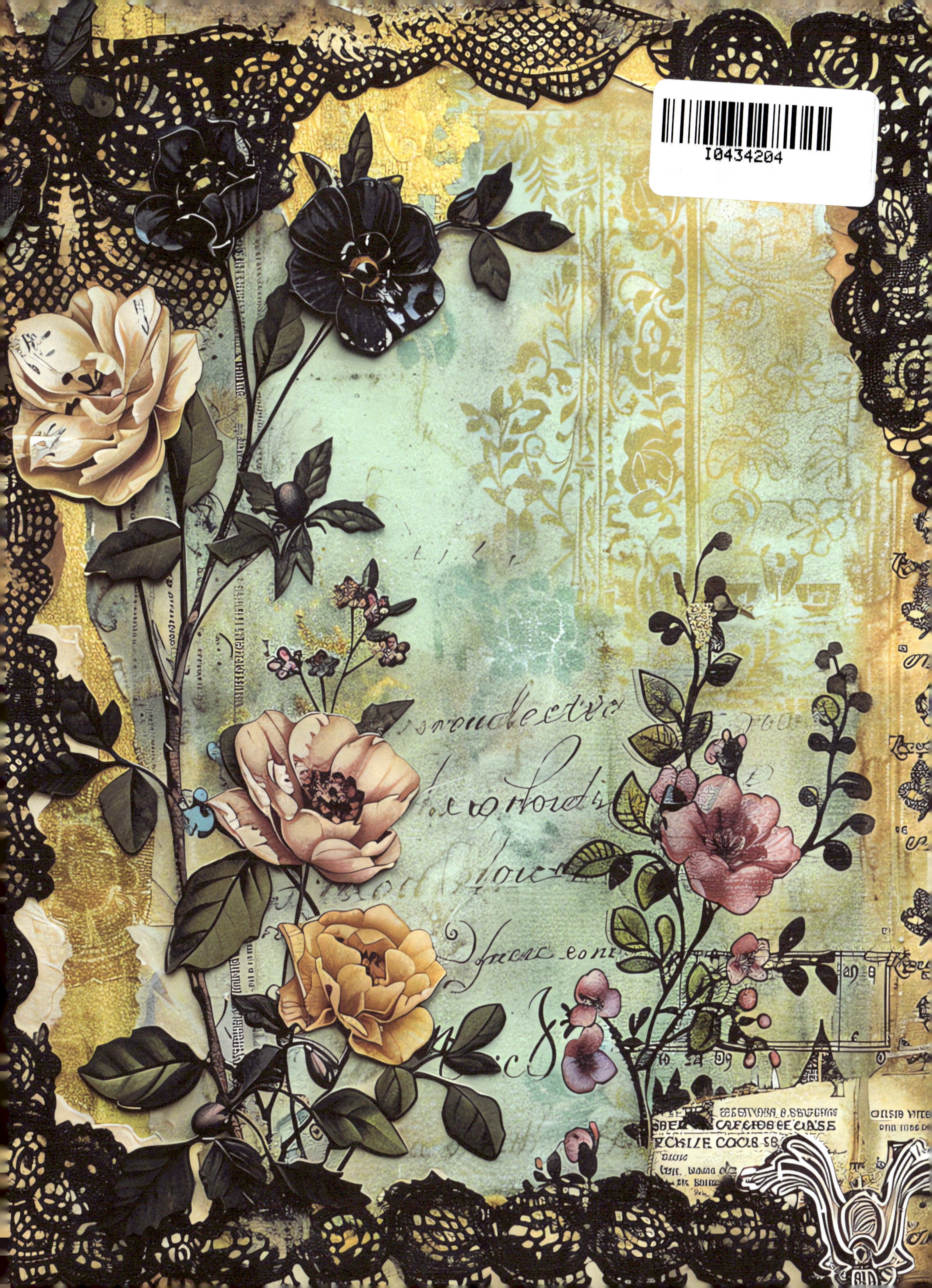

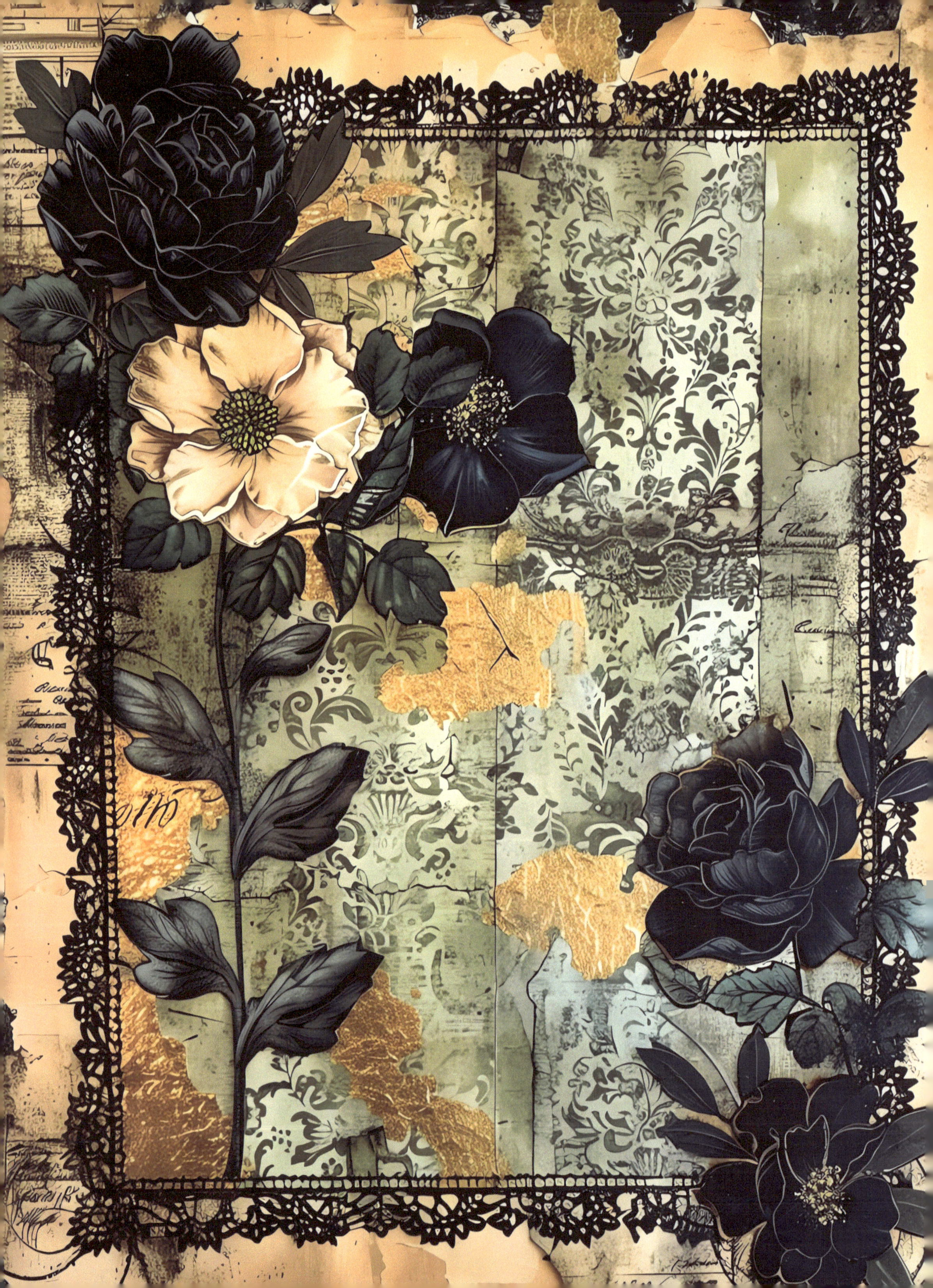

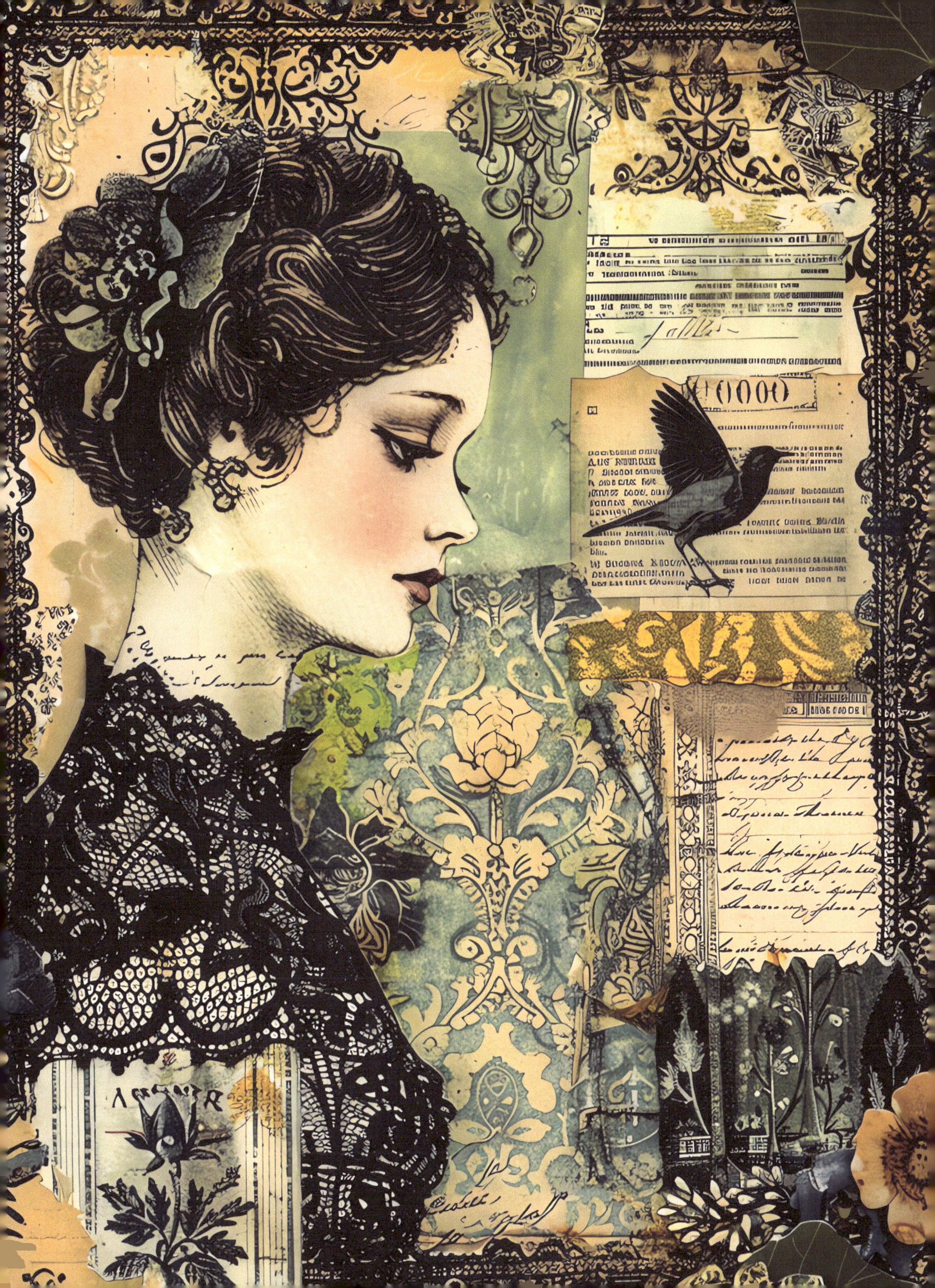

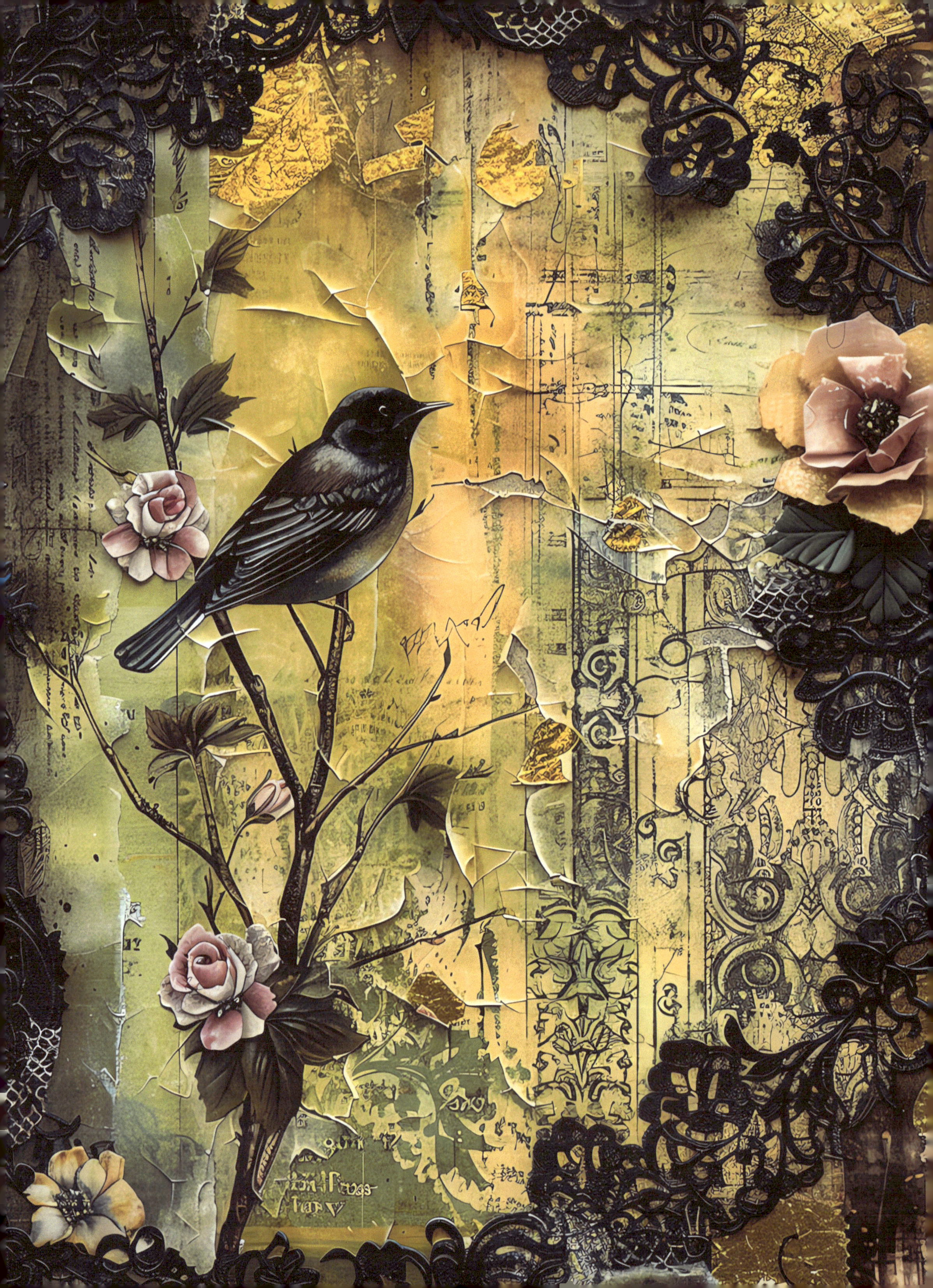

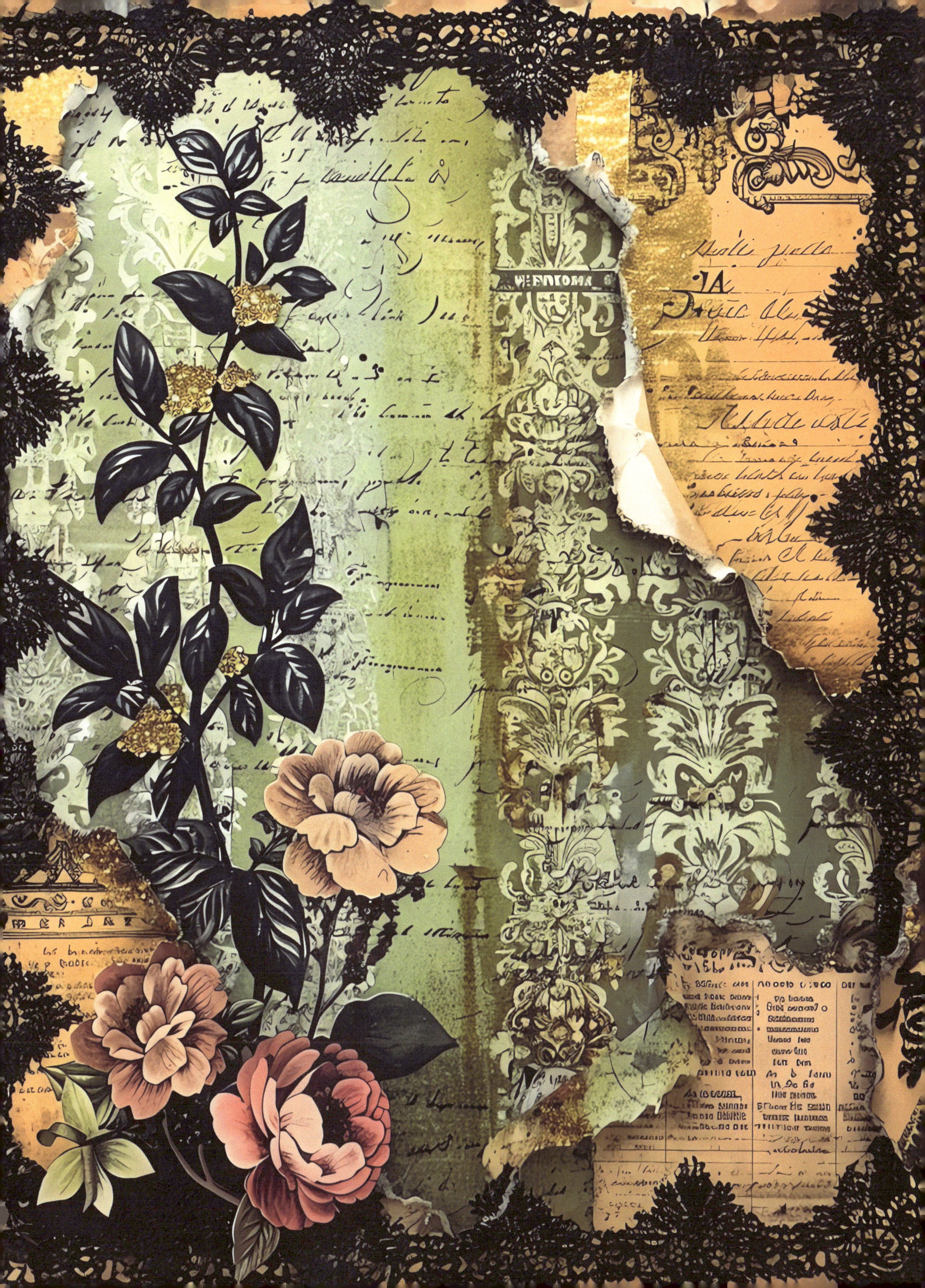

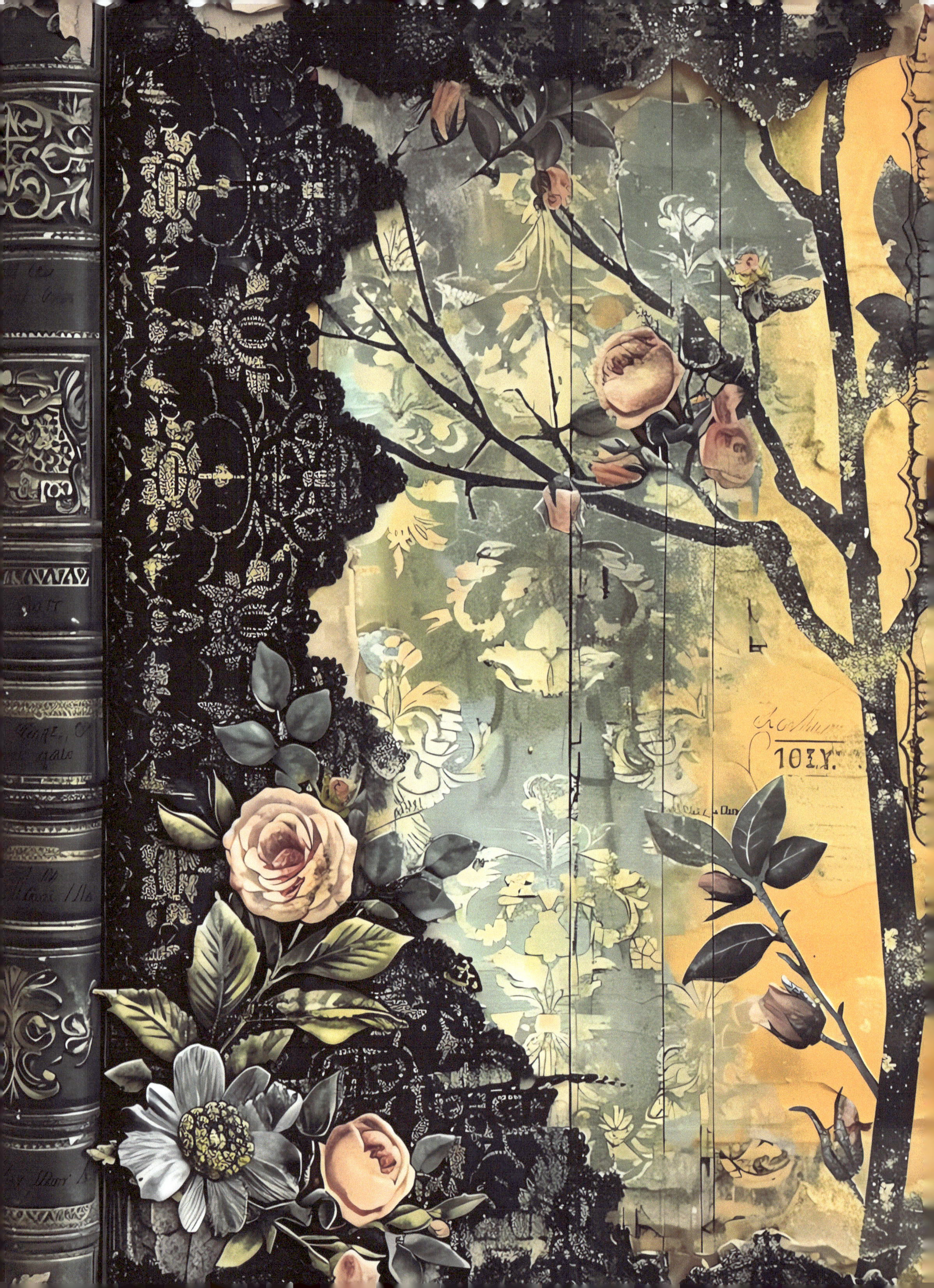

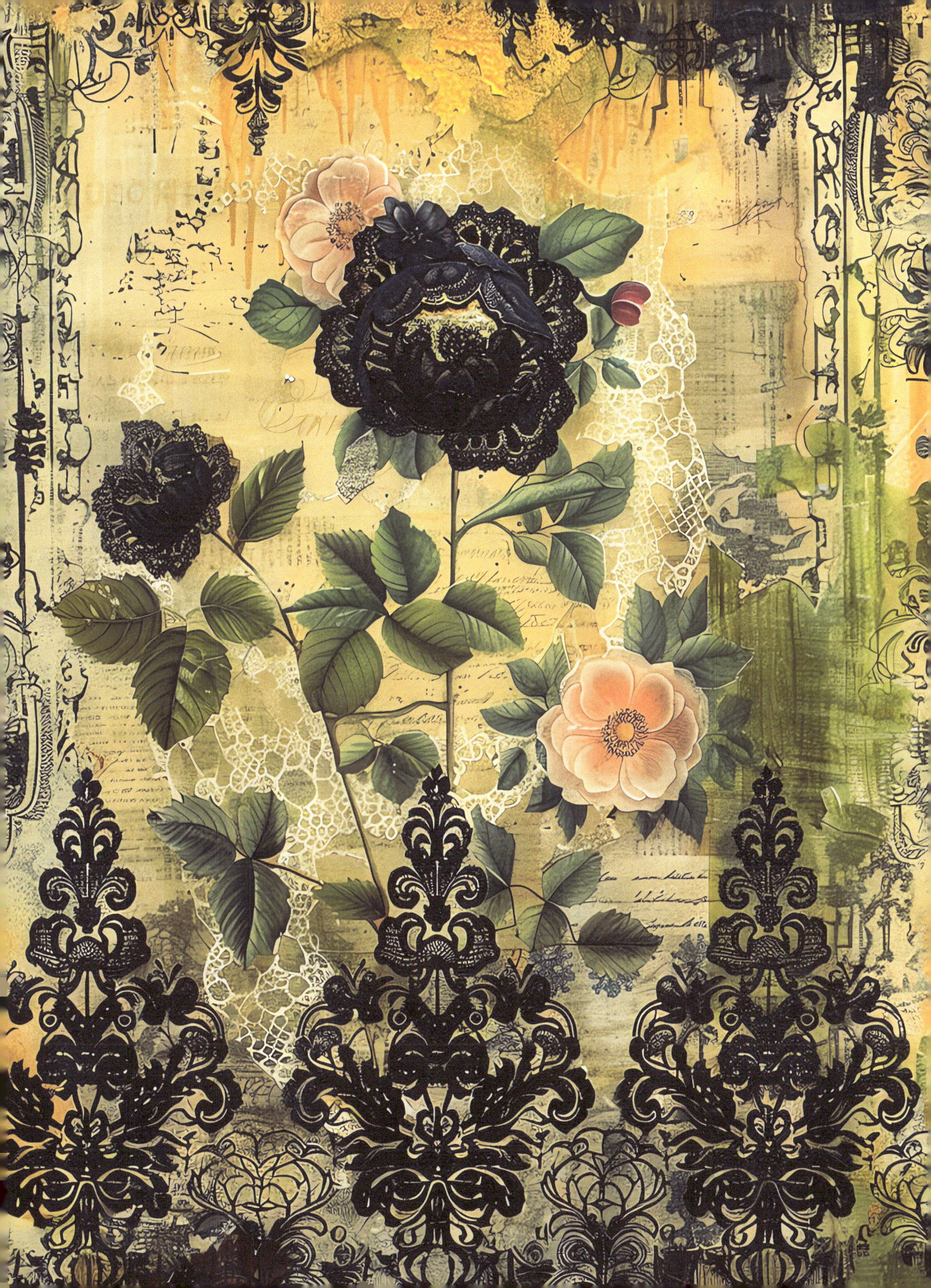

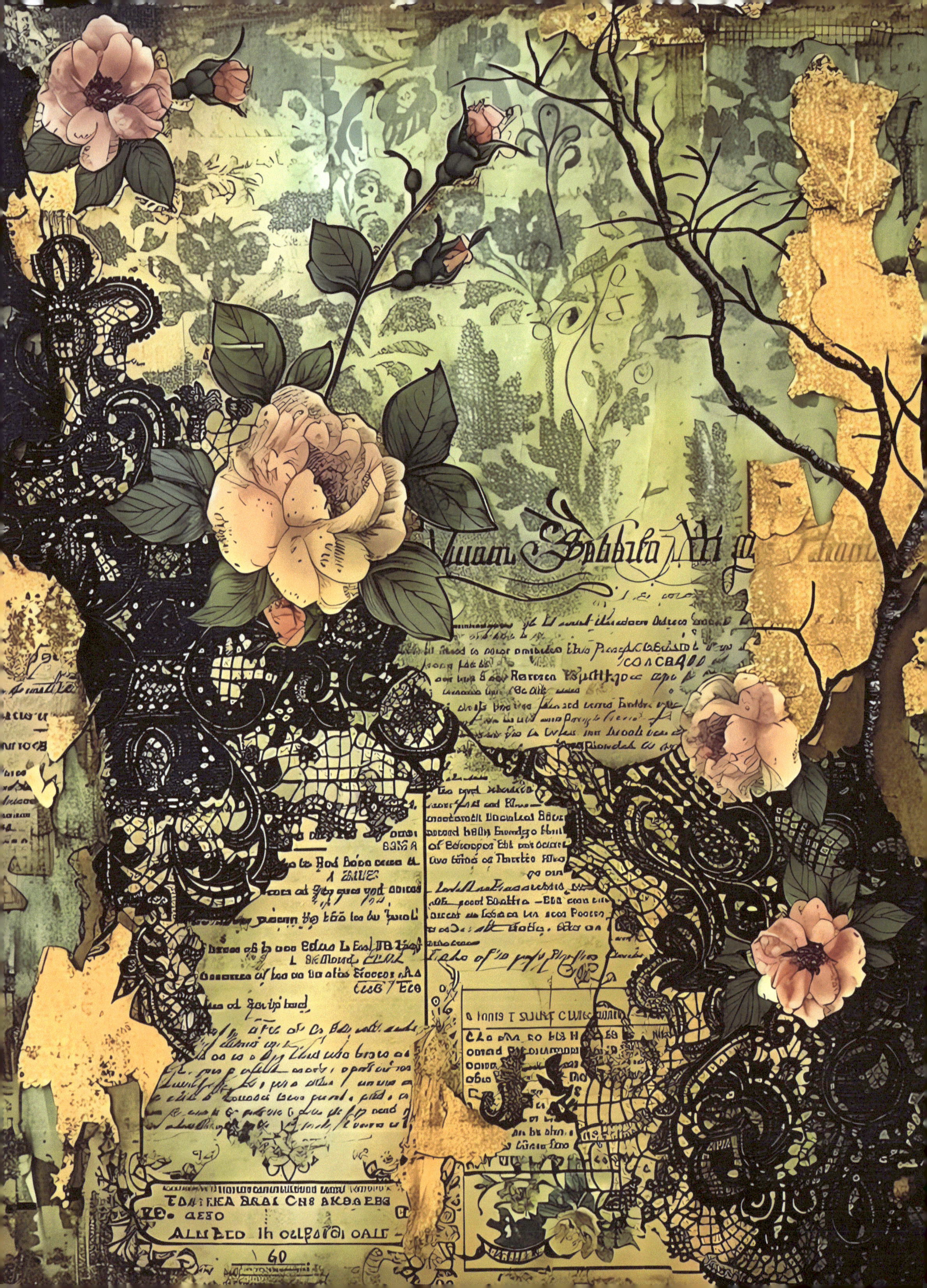

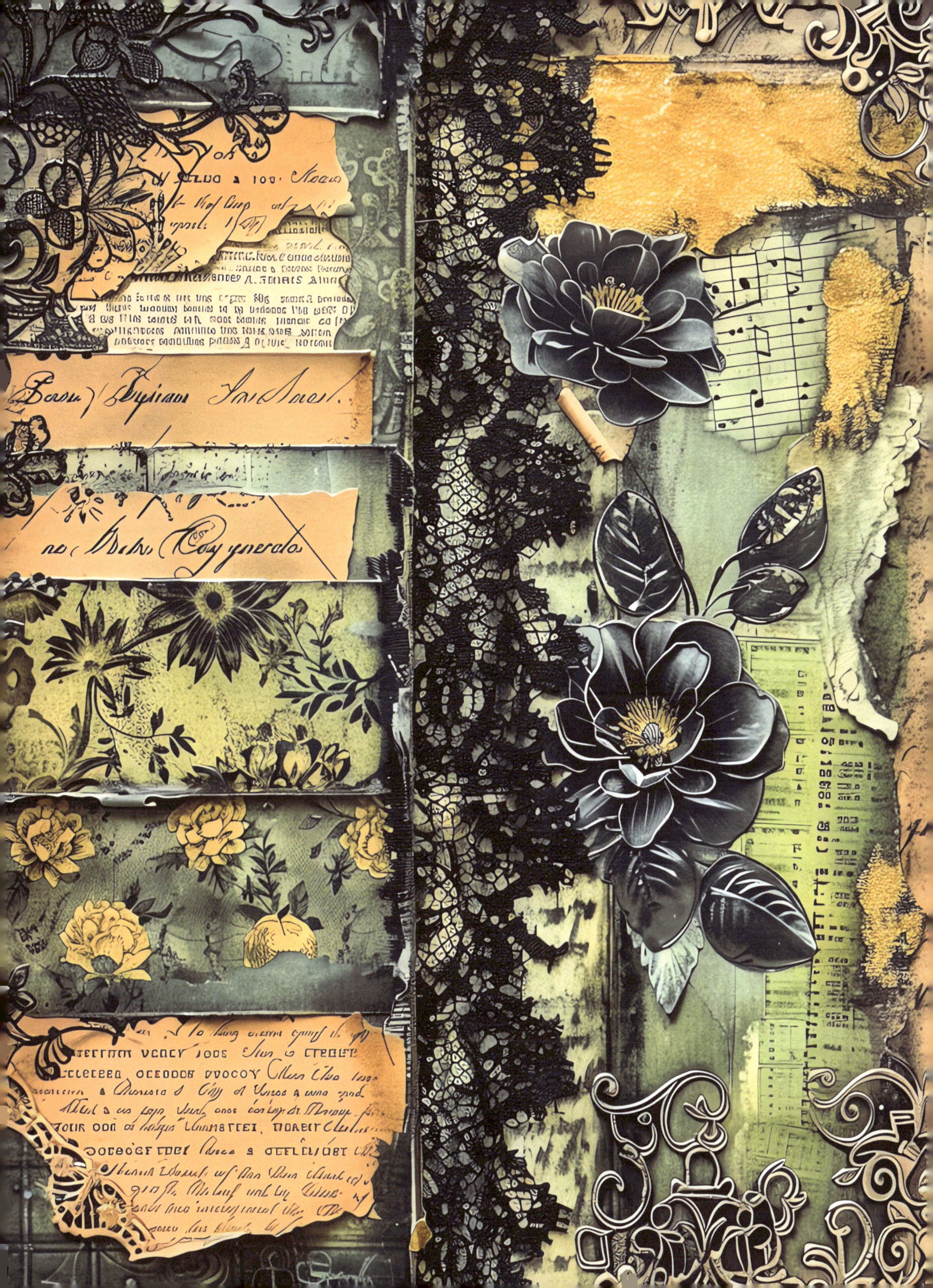

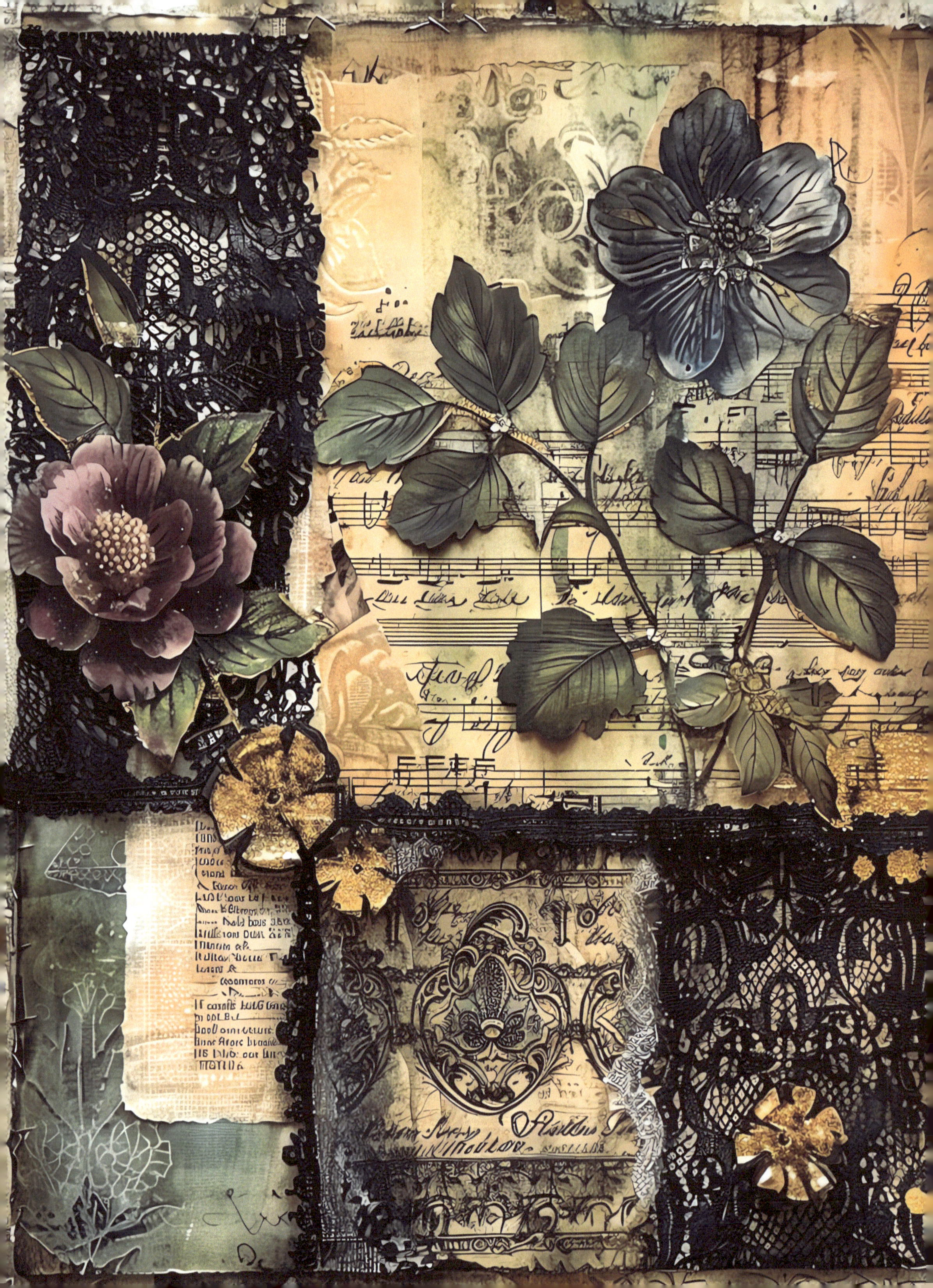

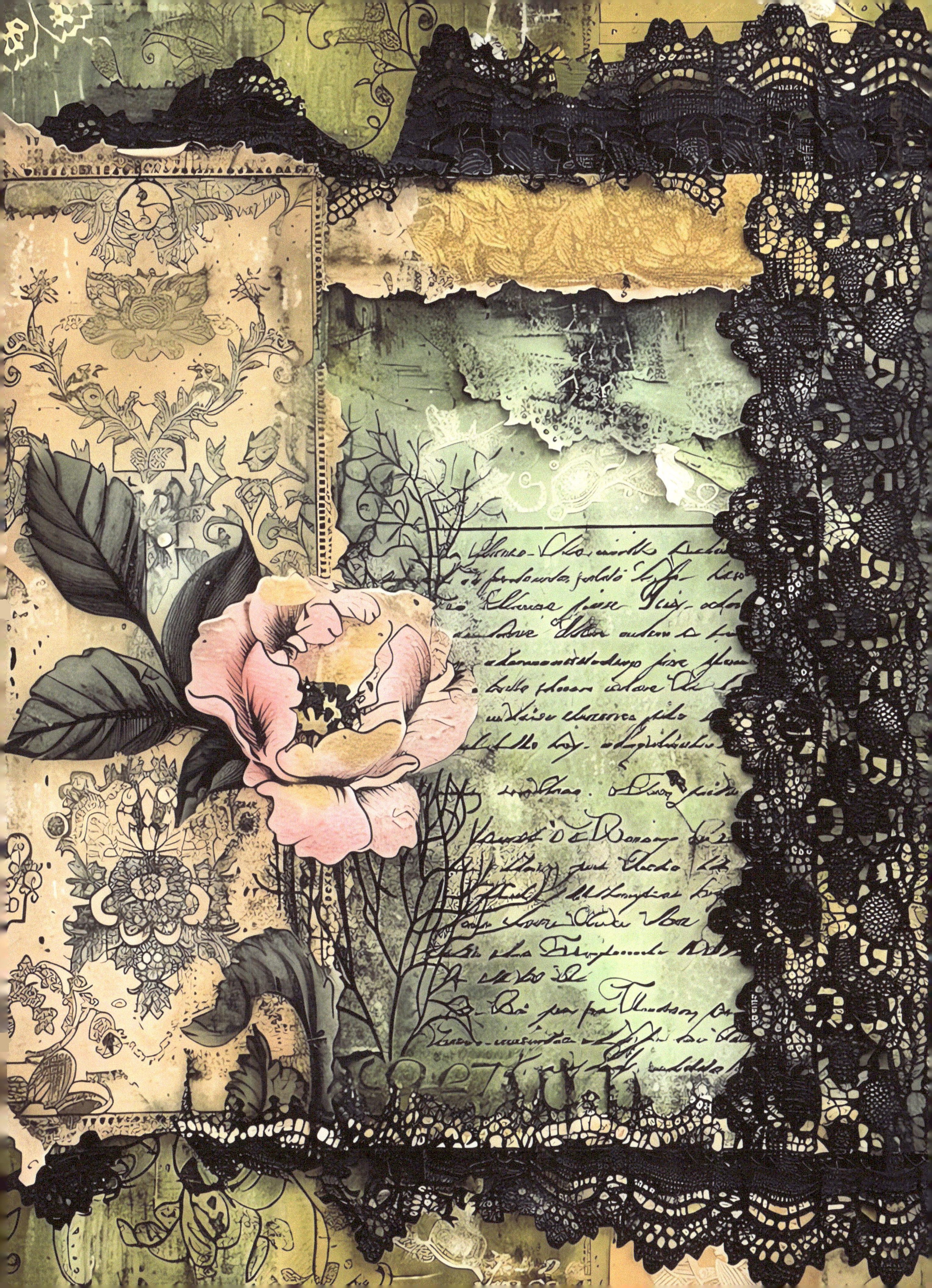

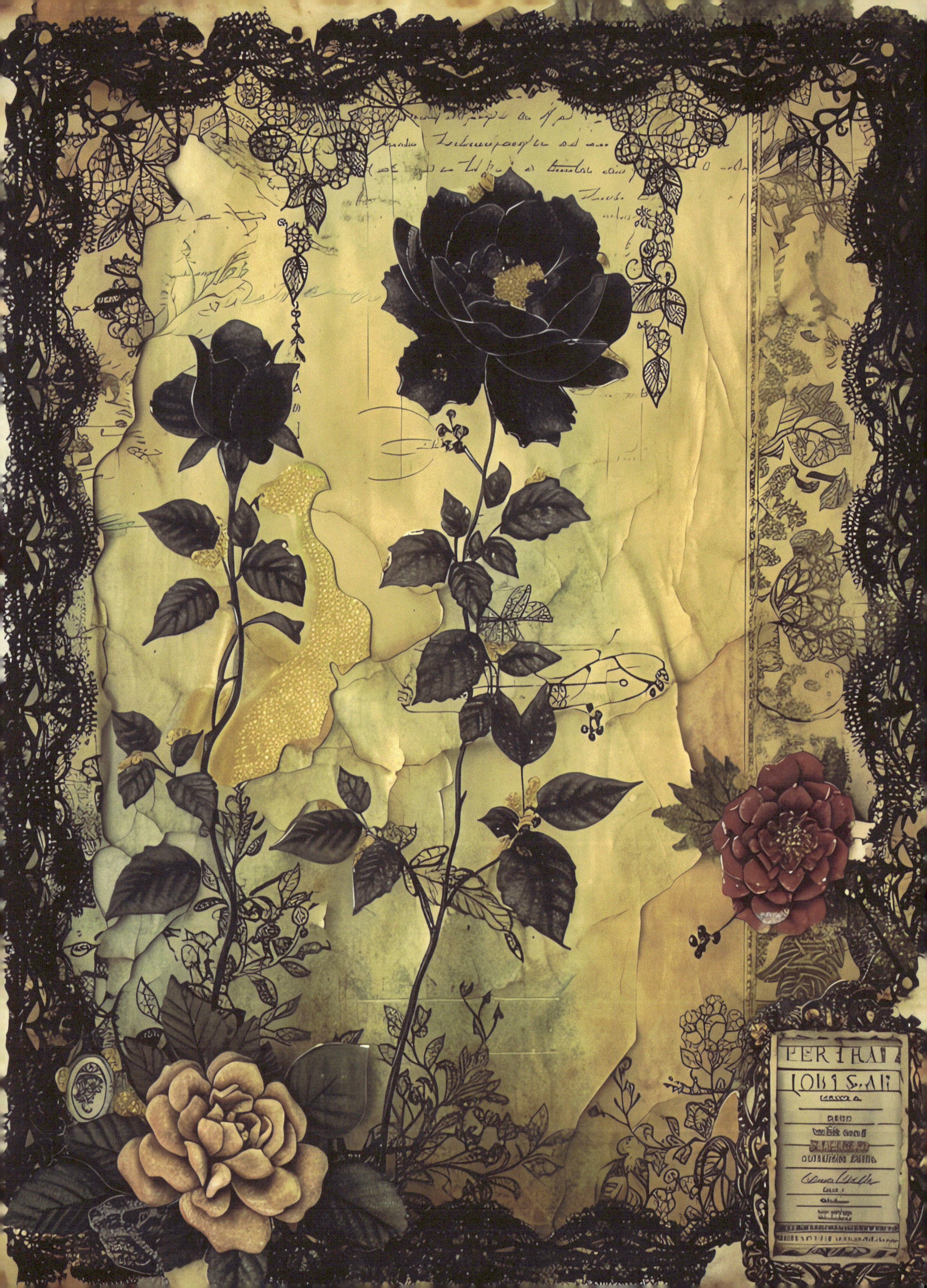

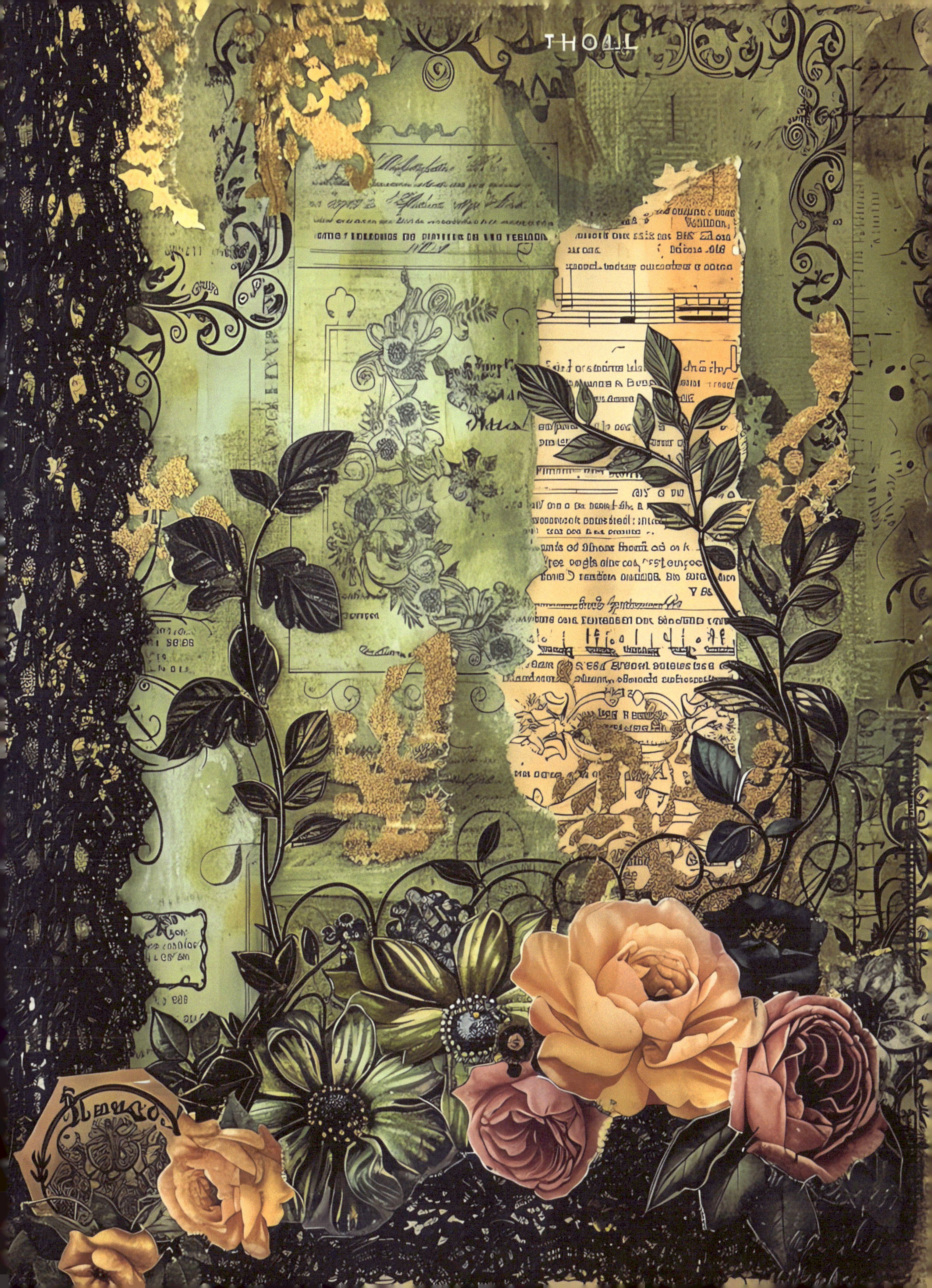
THOLL

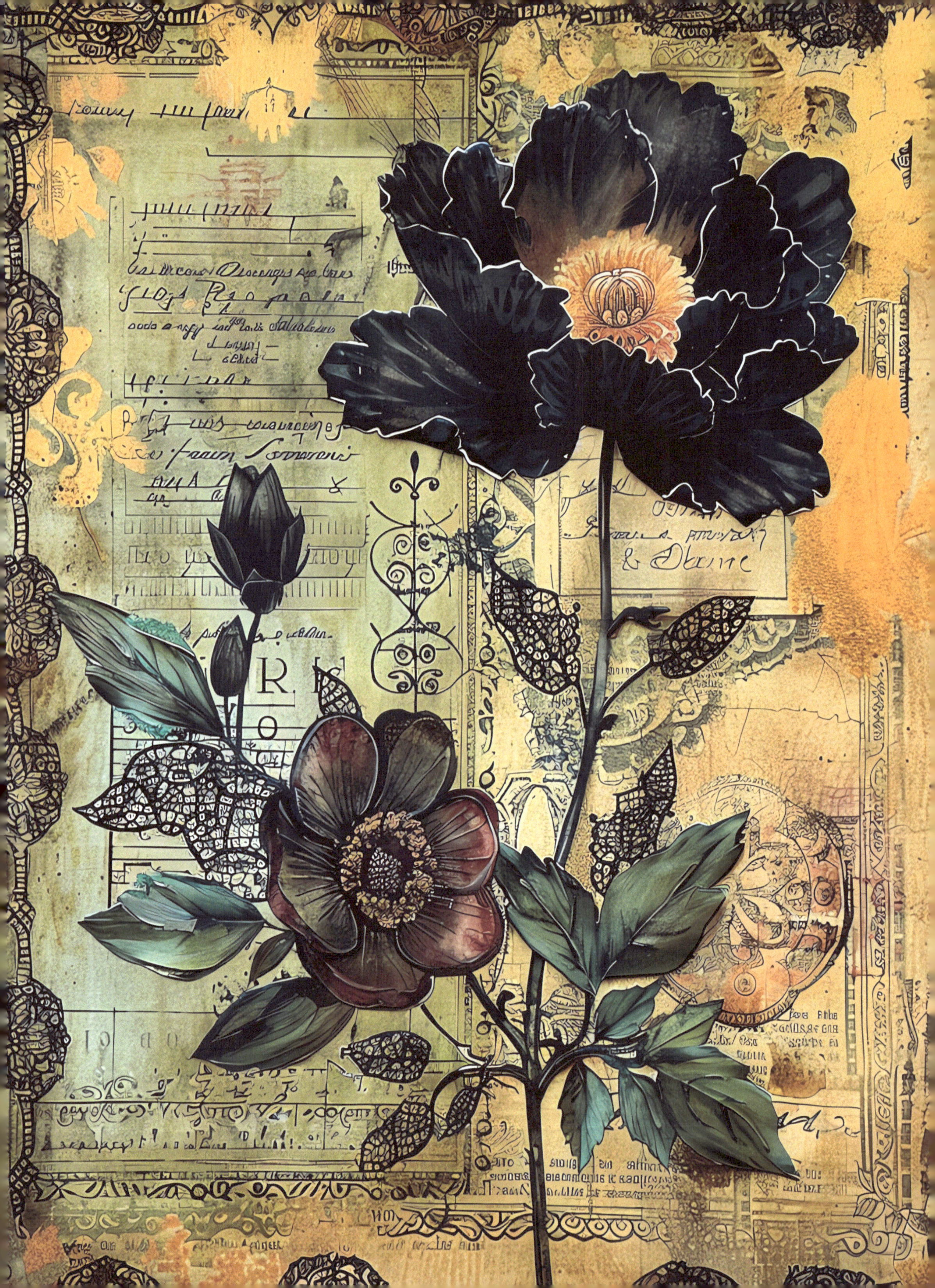

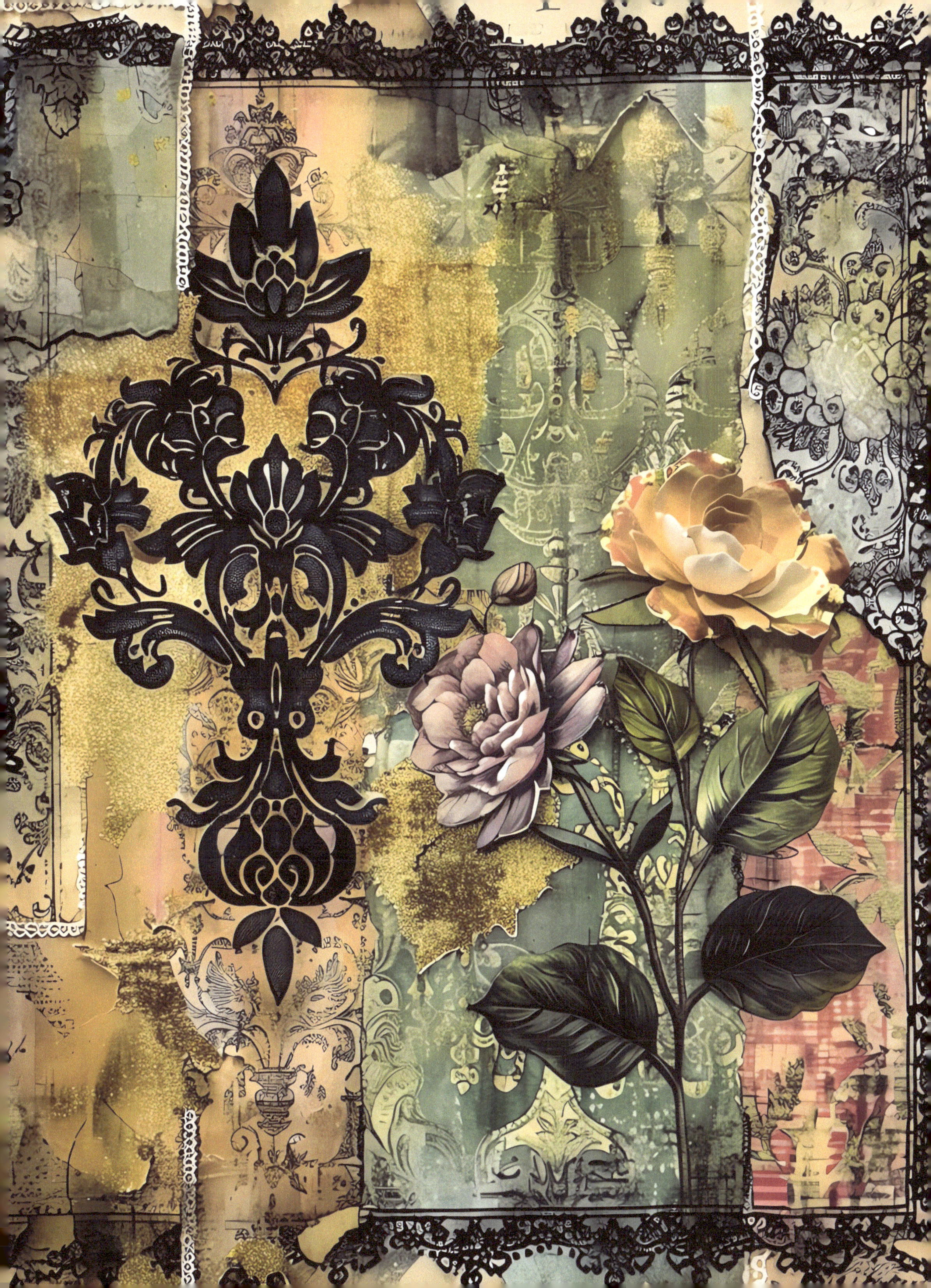

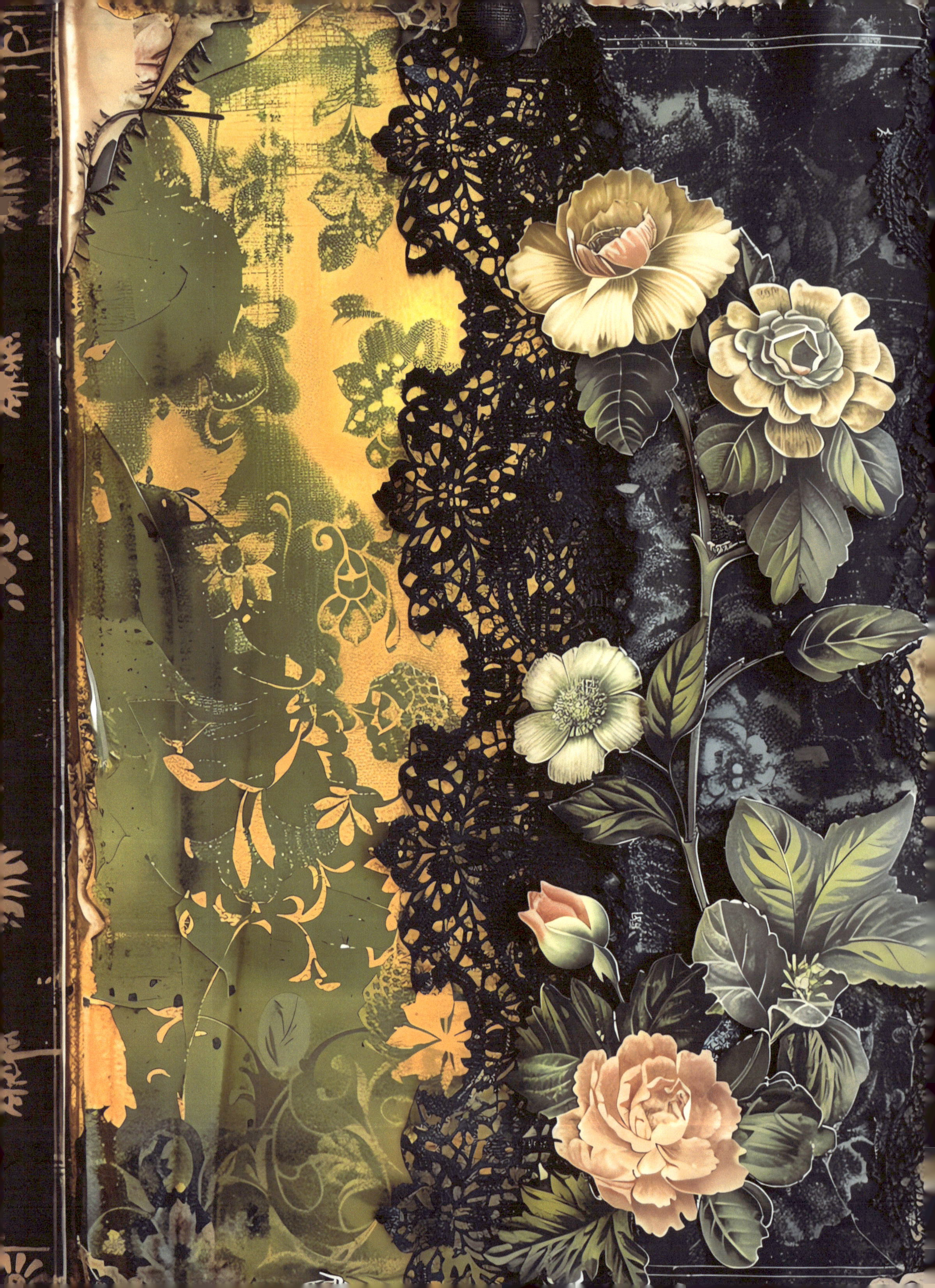

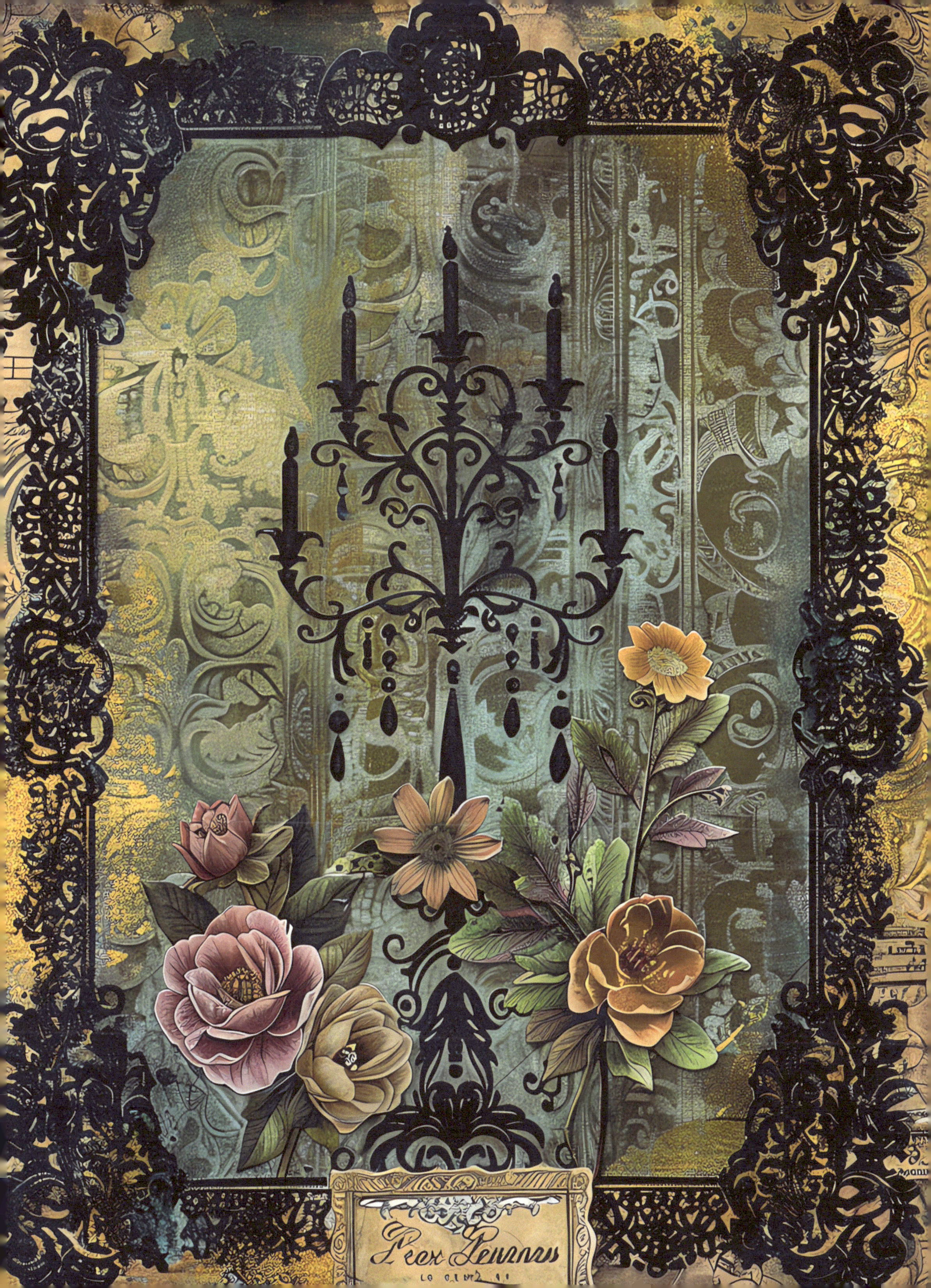

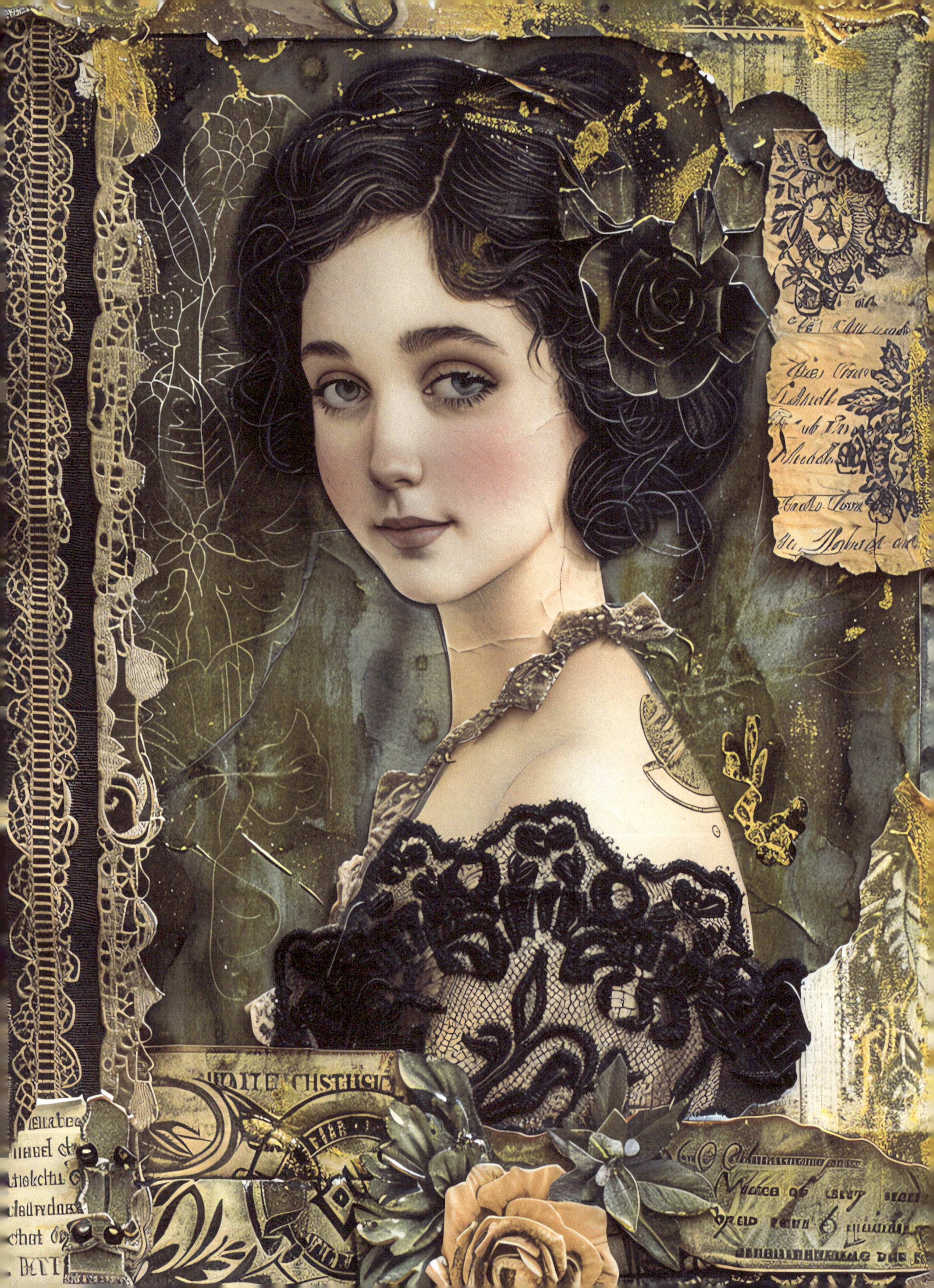

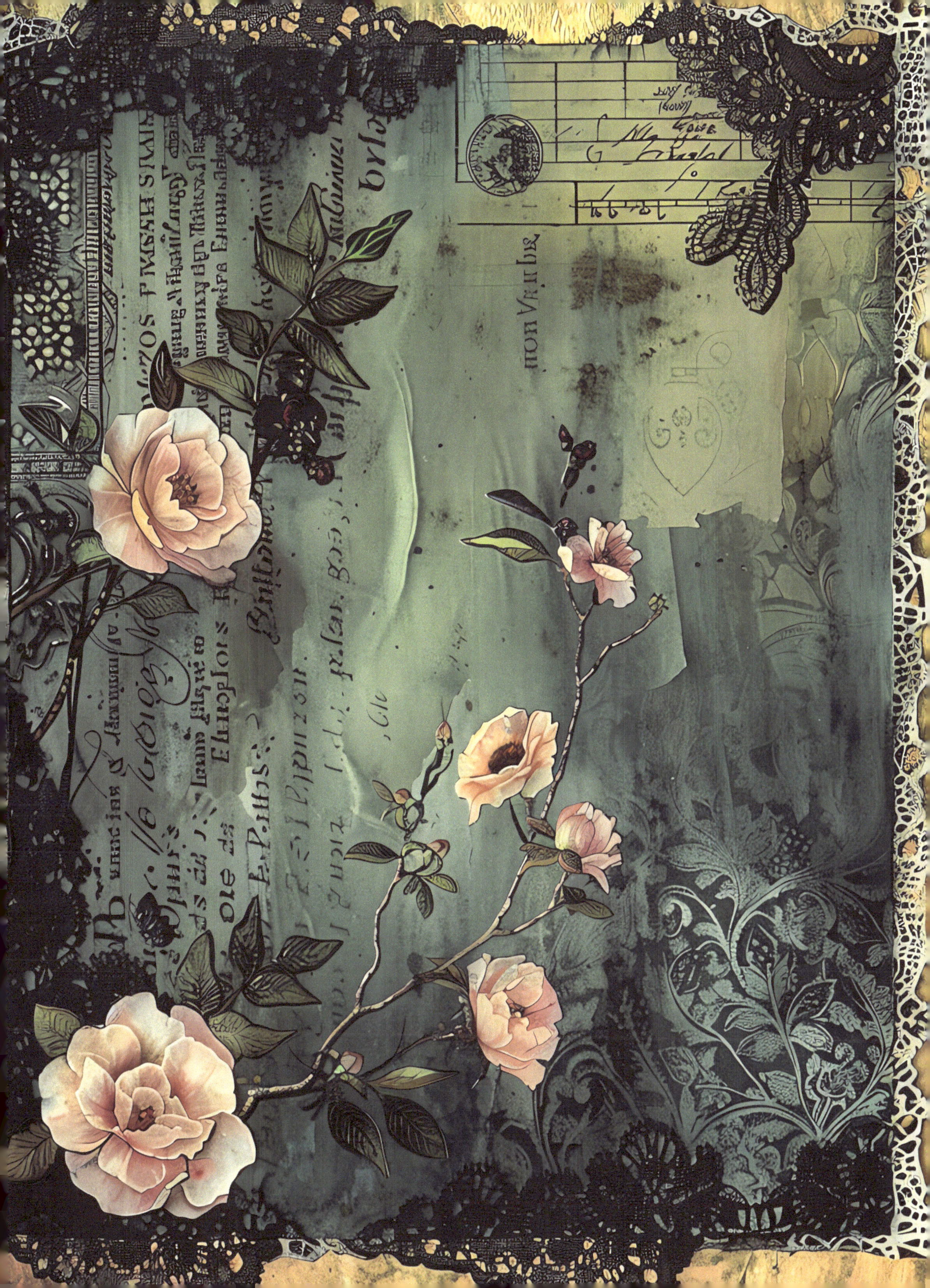

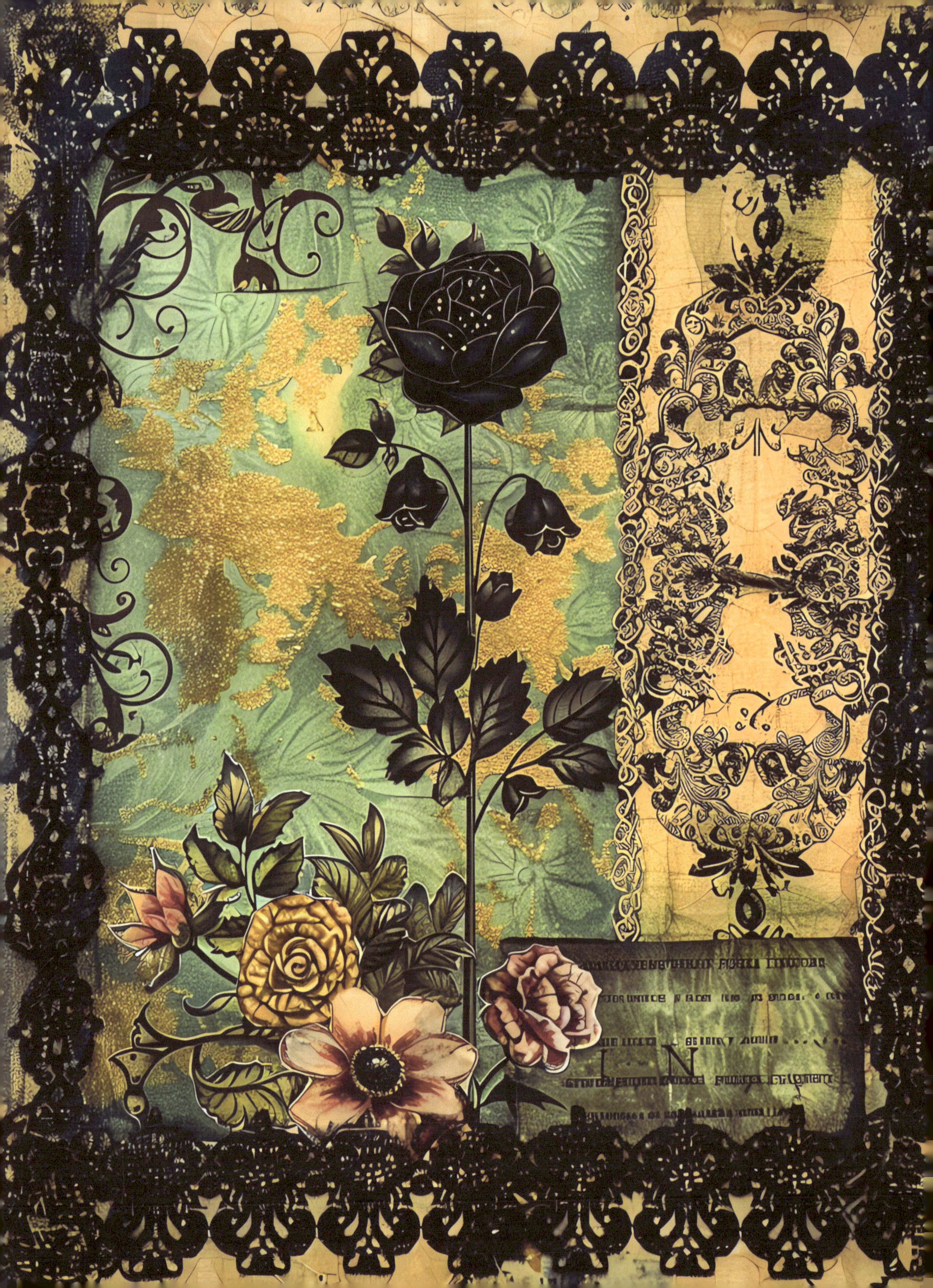

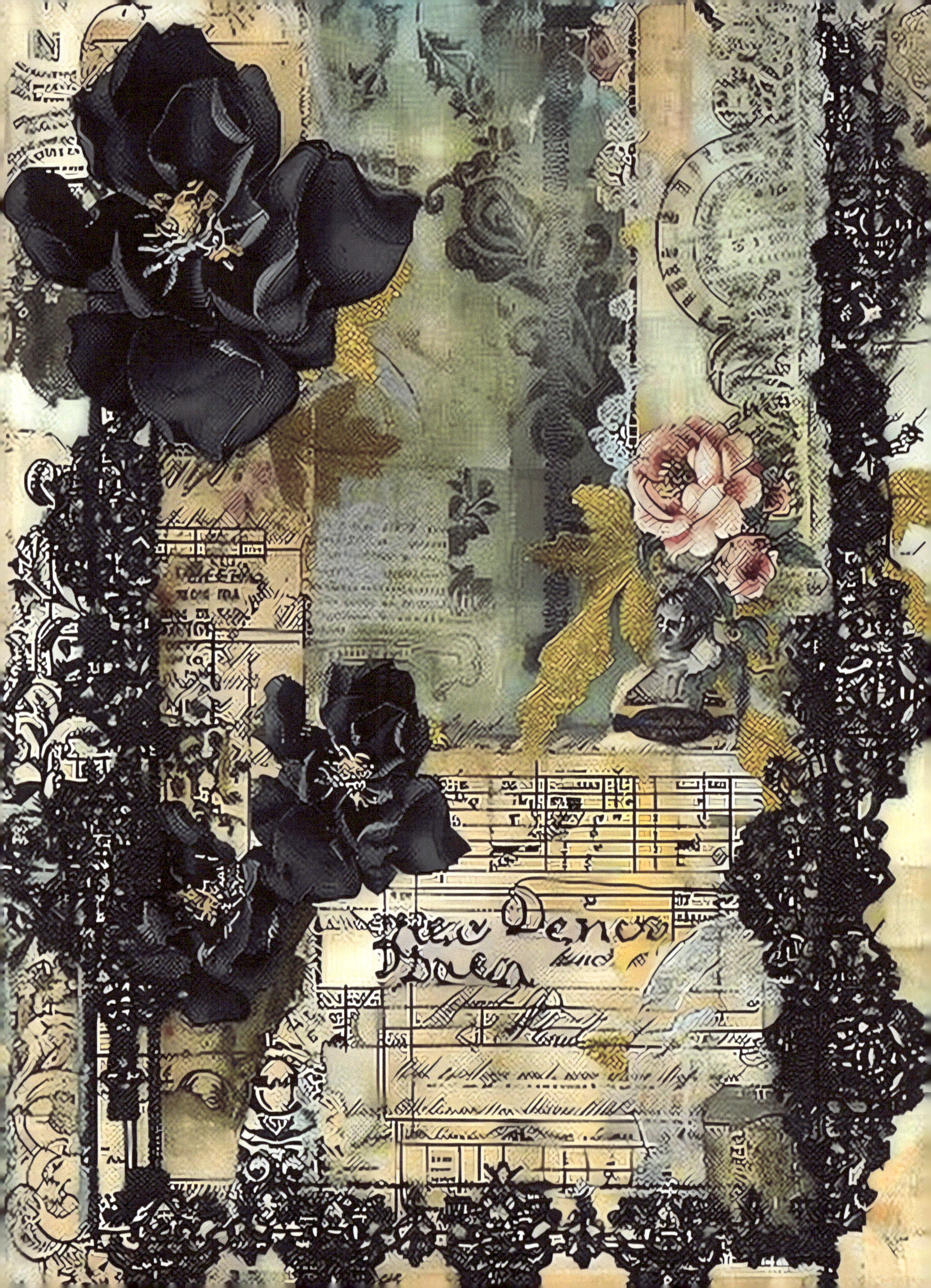

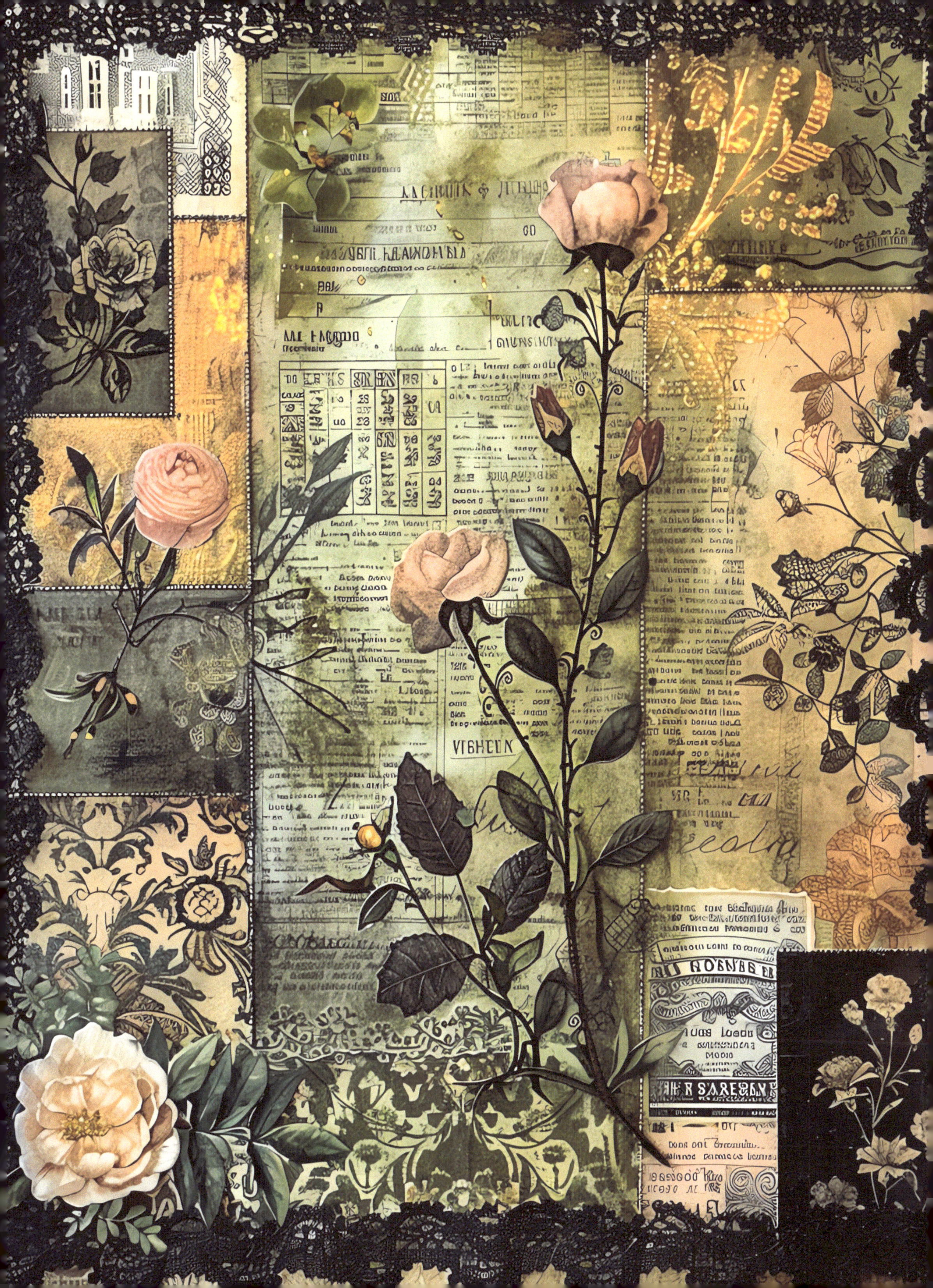

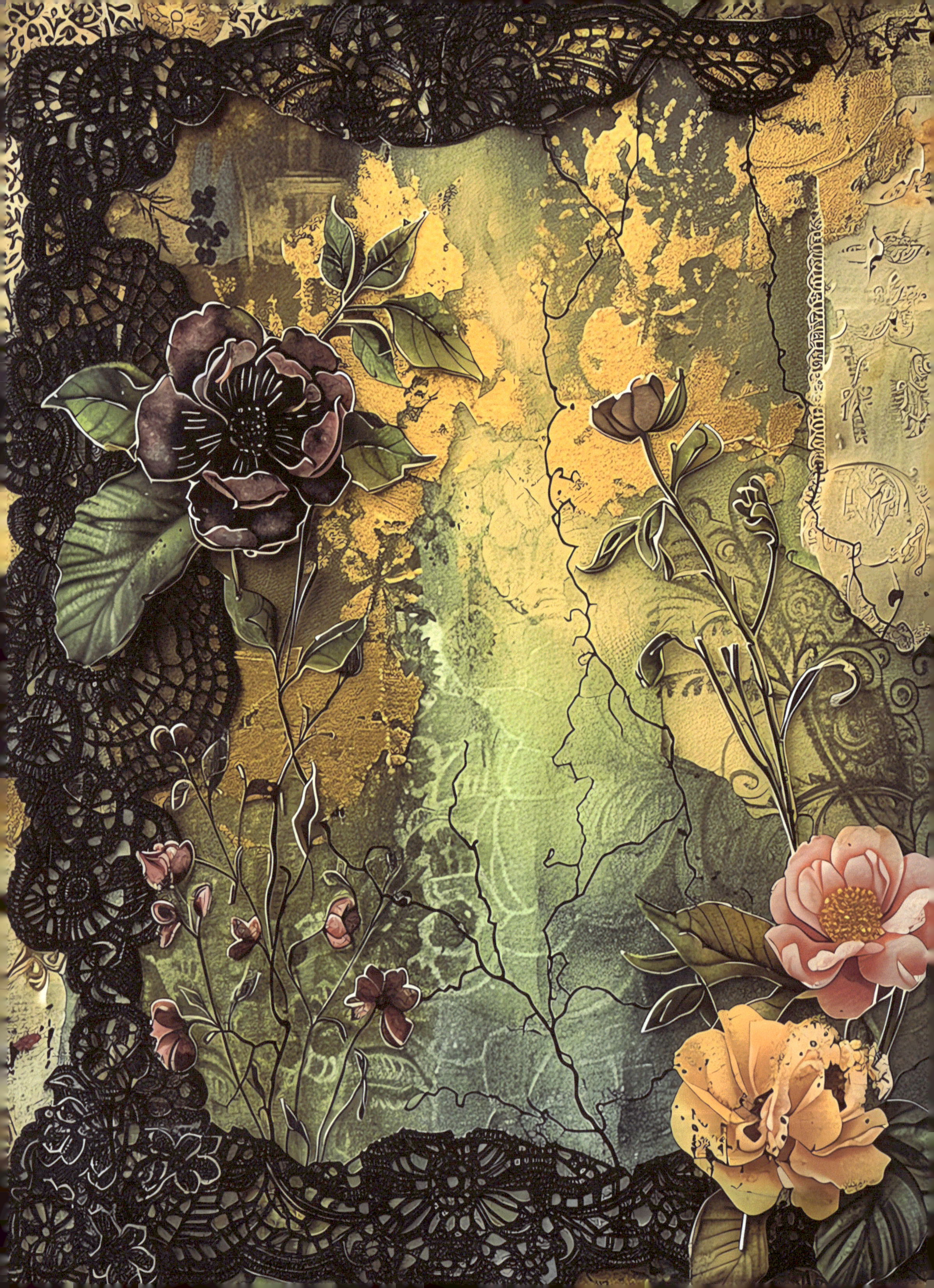

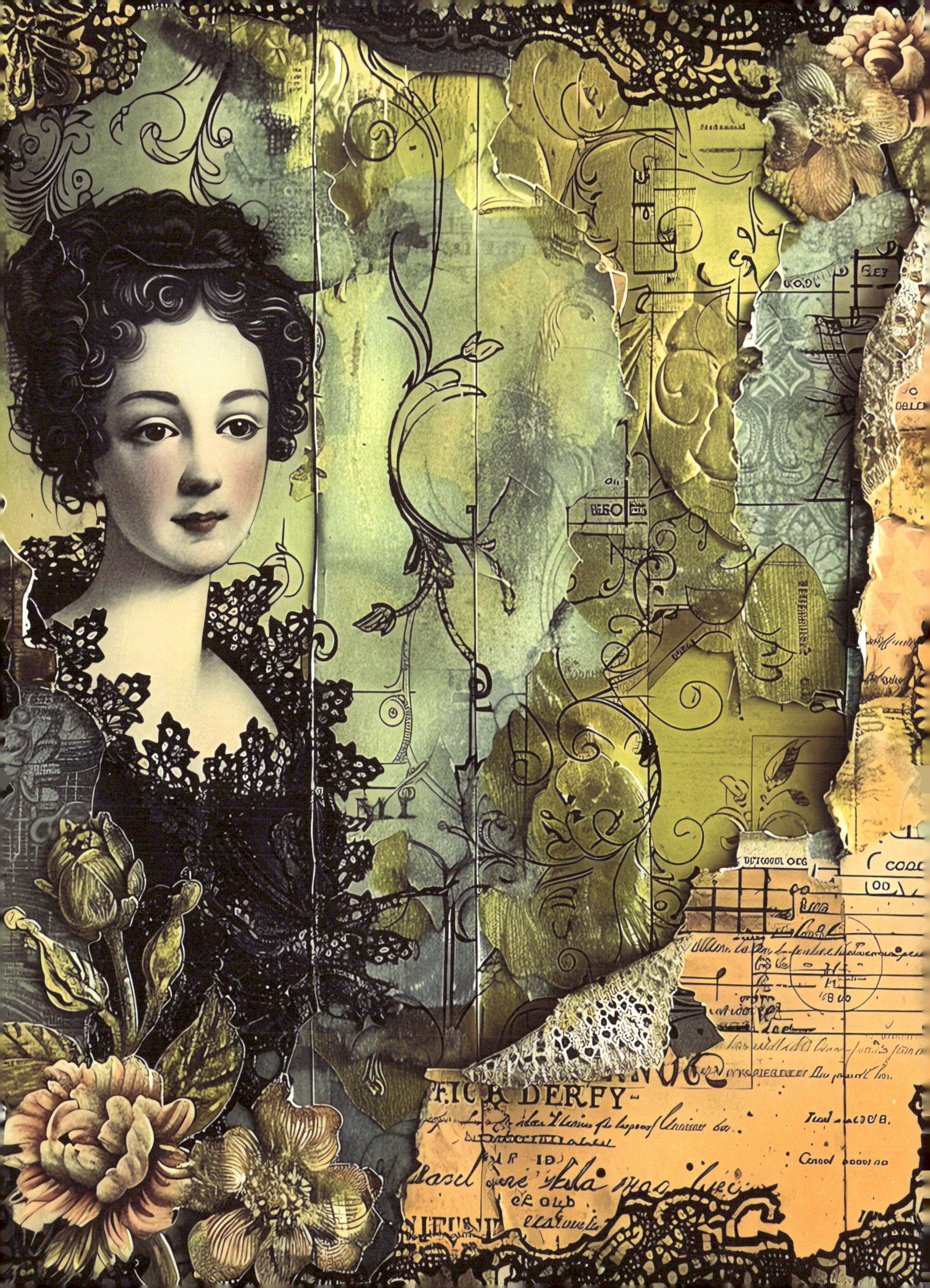

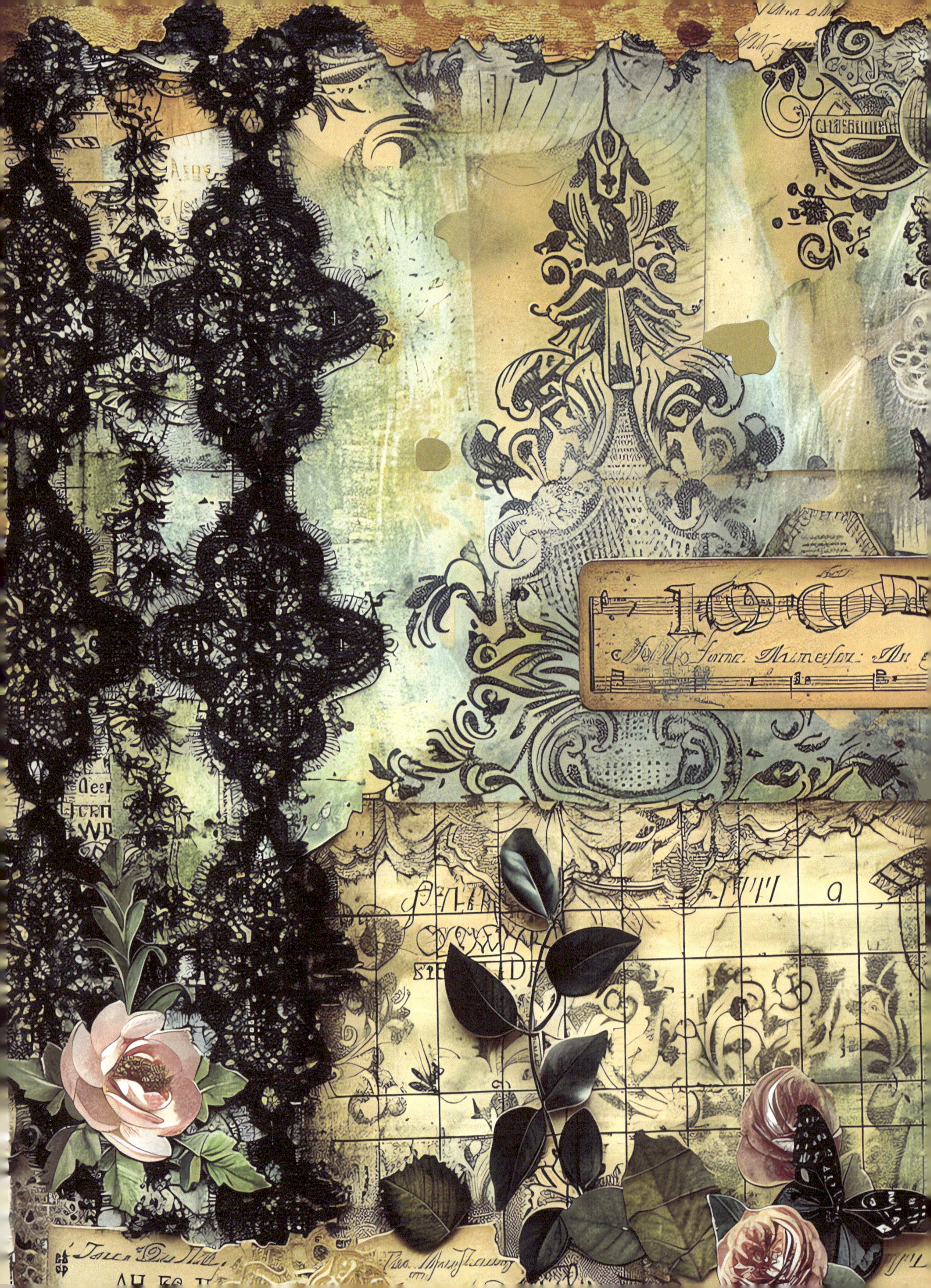

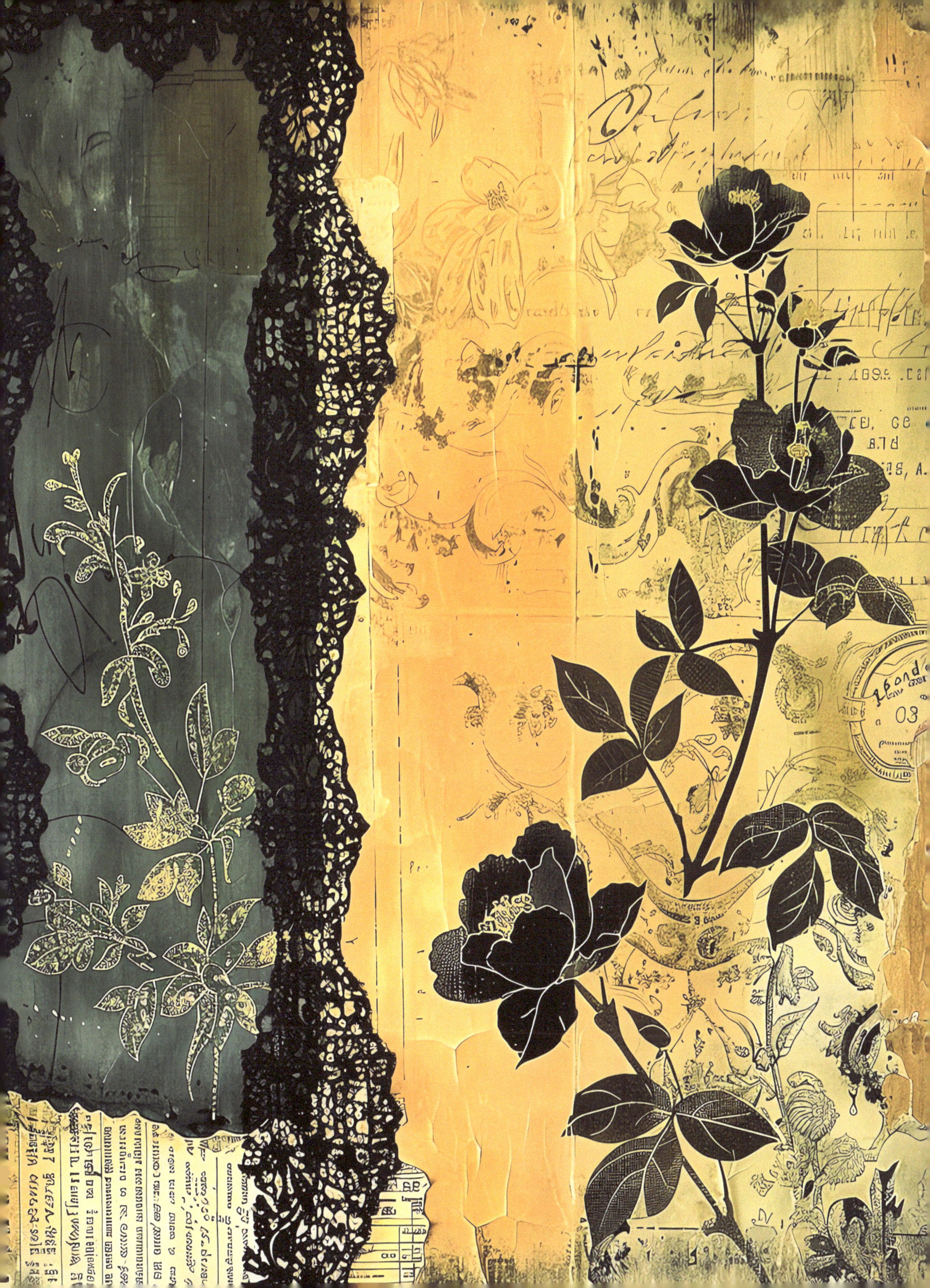

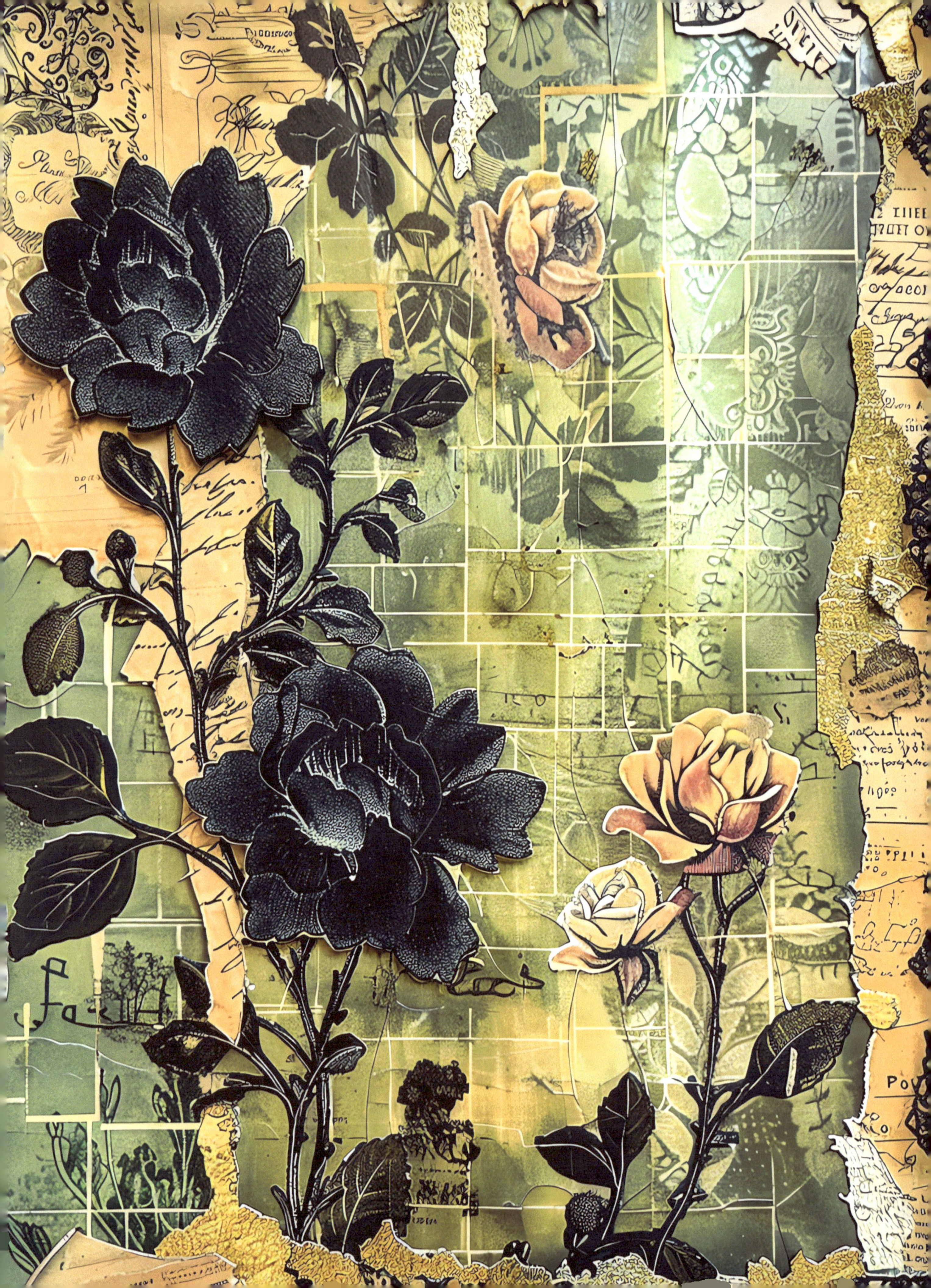

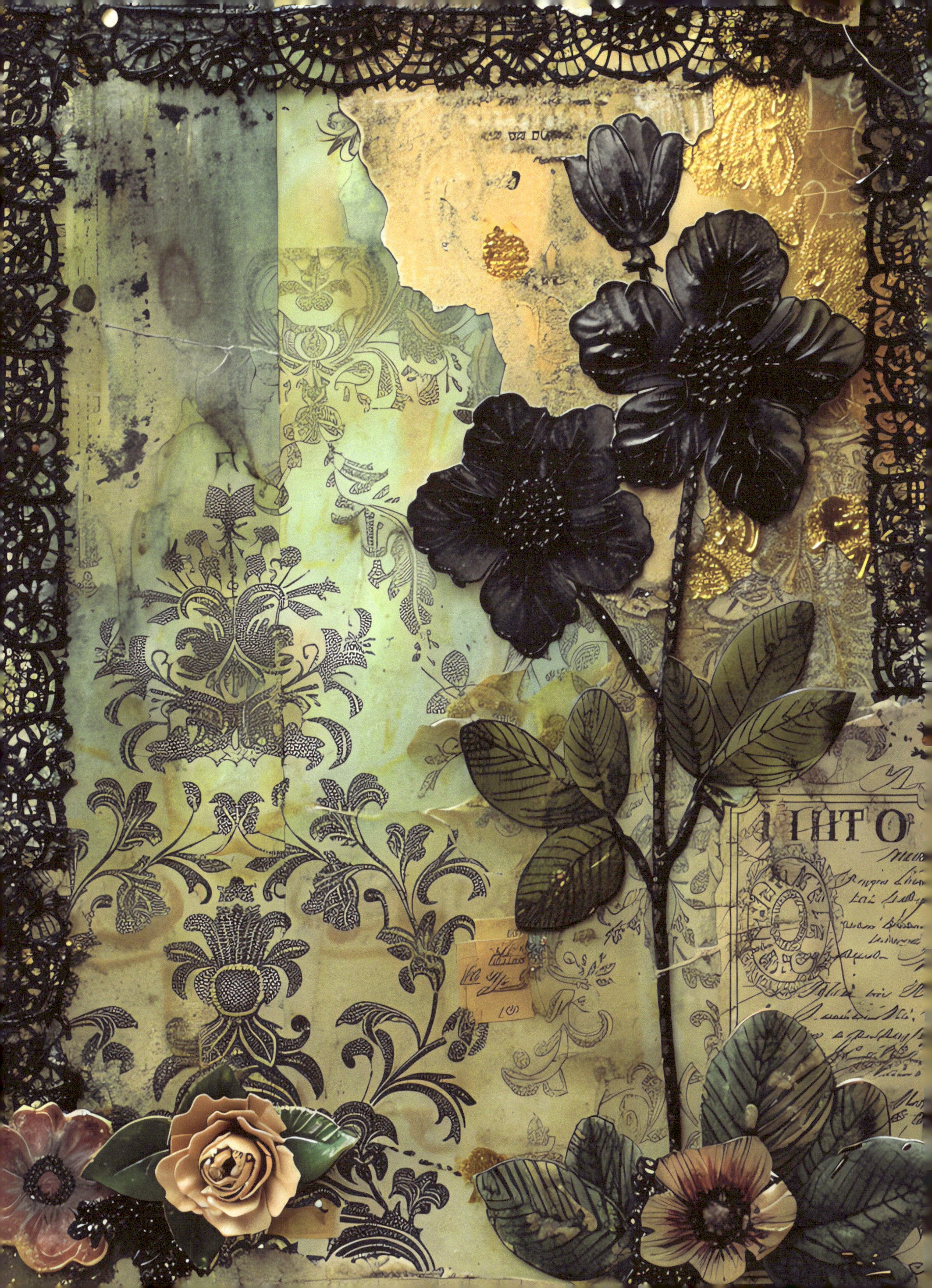

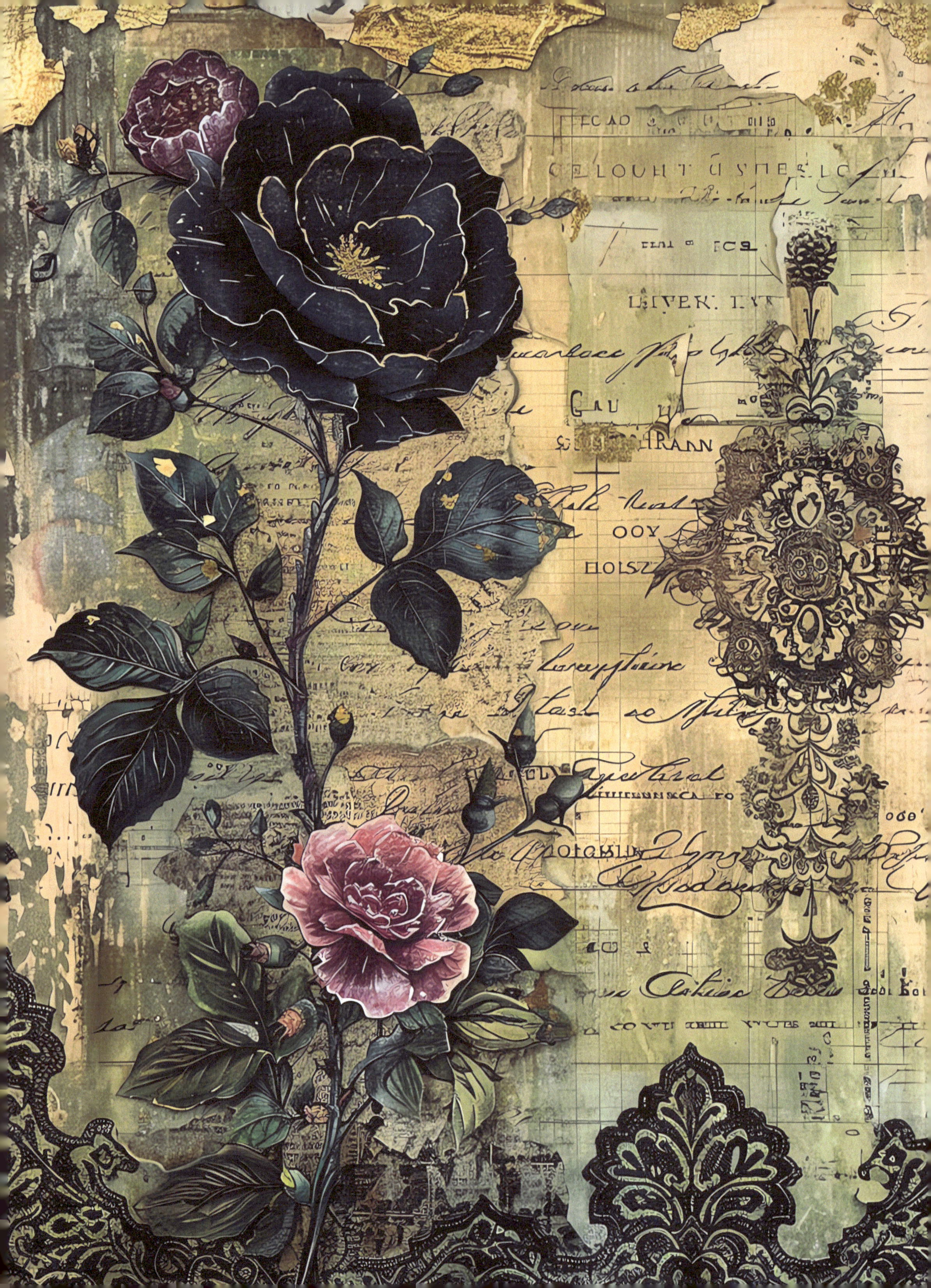

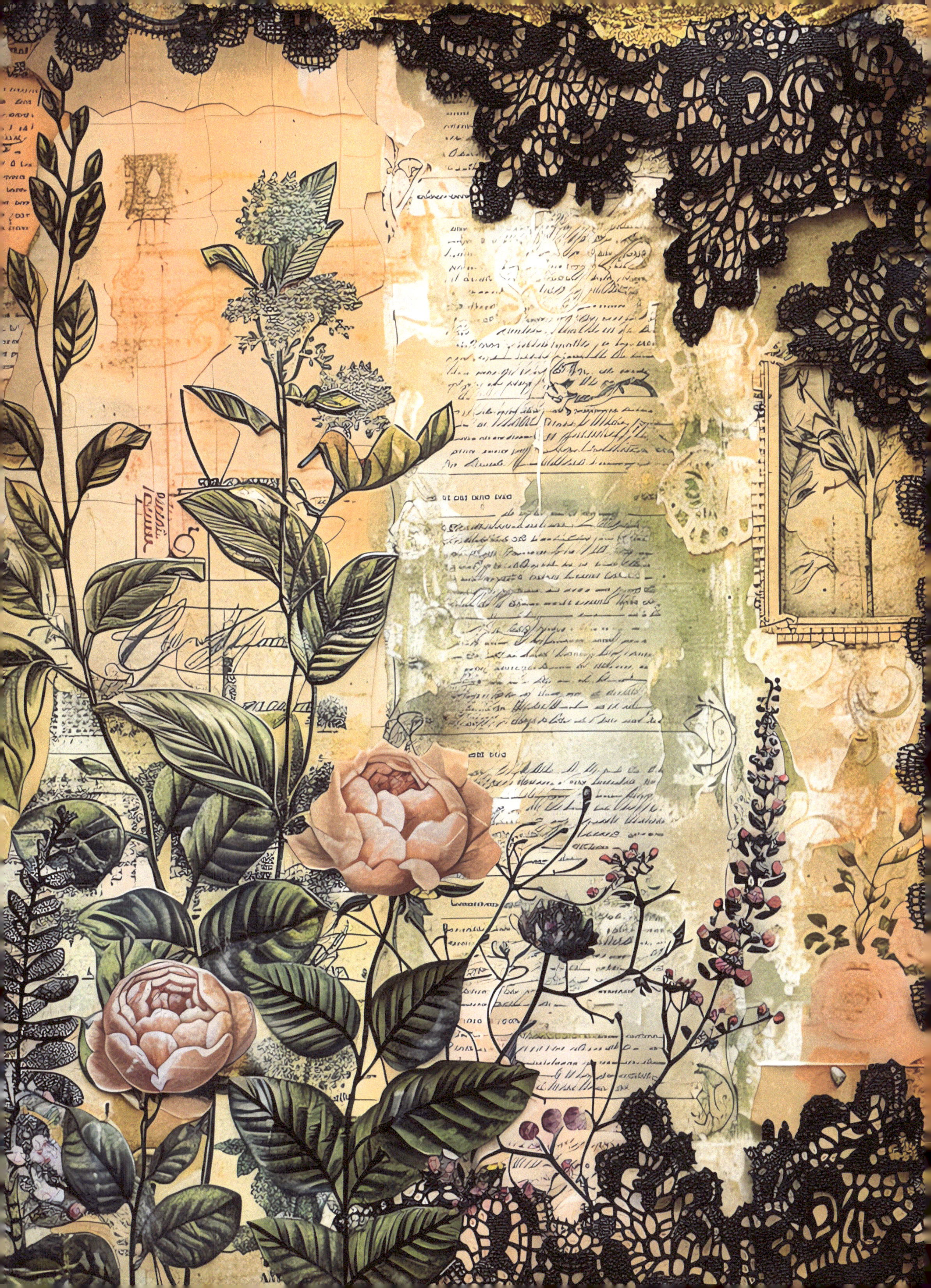

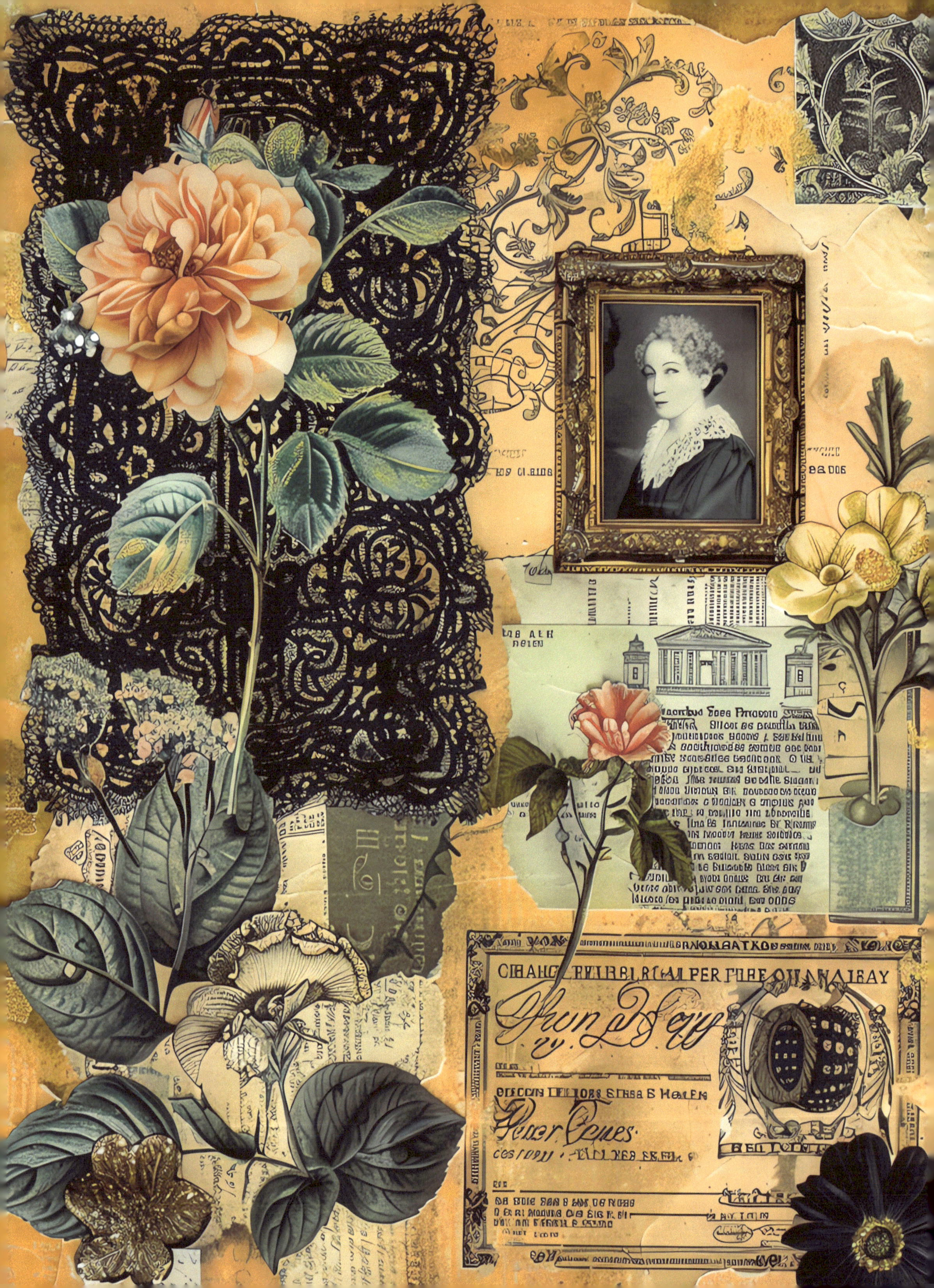

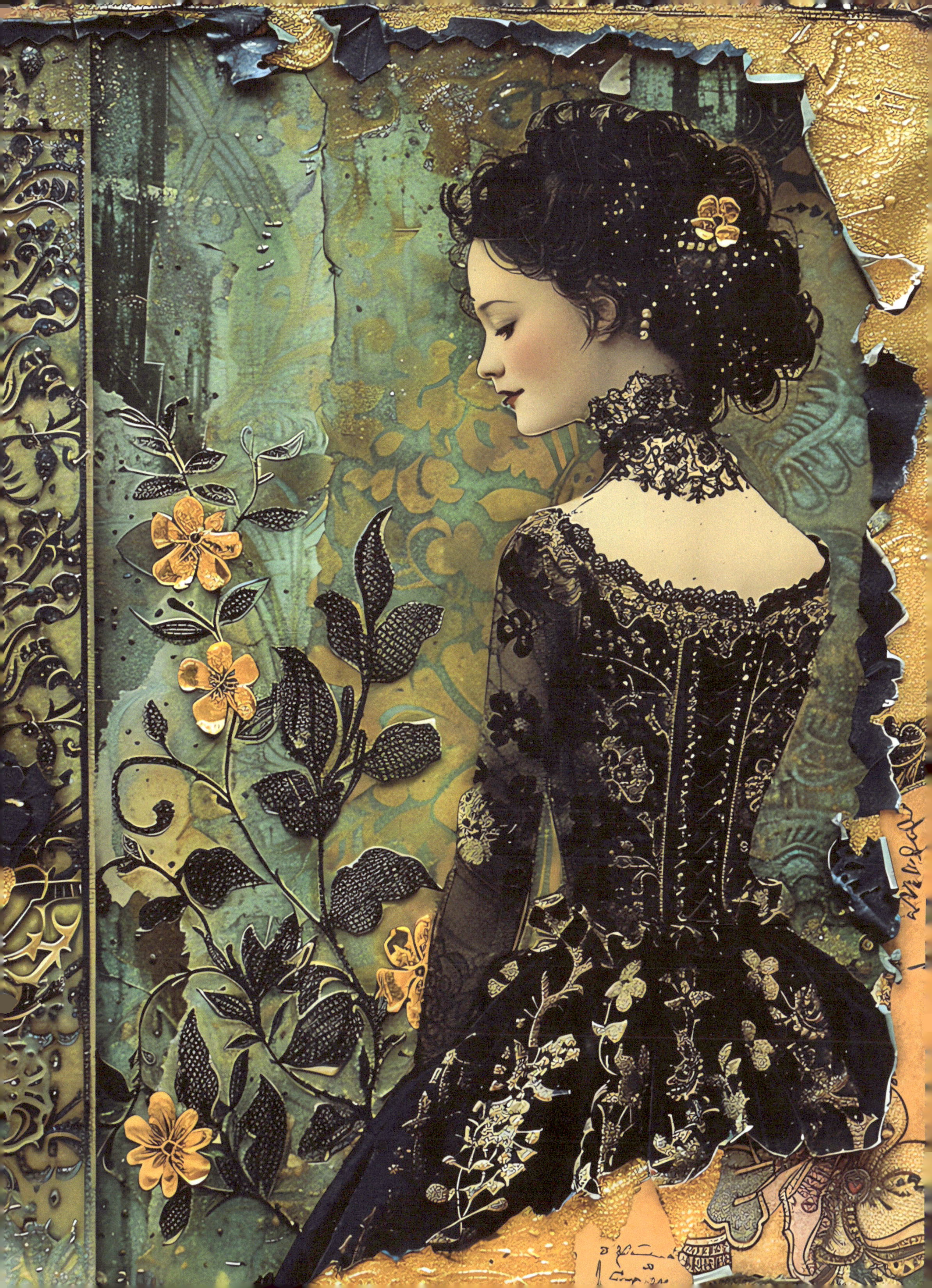

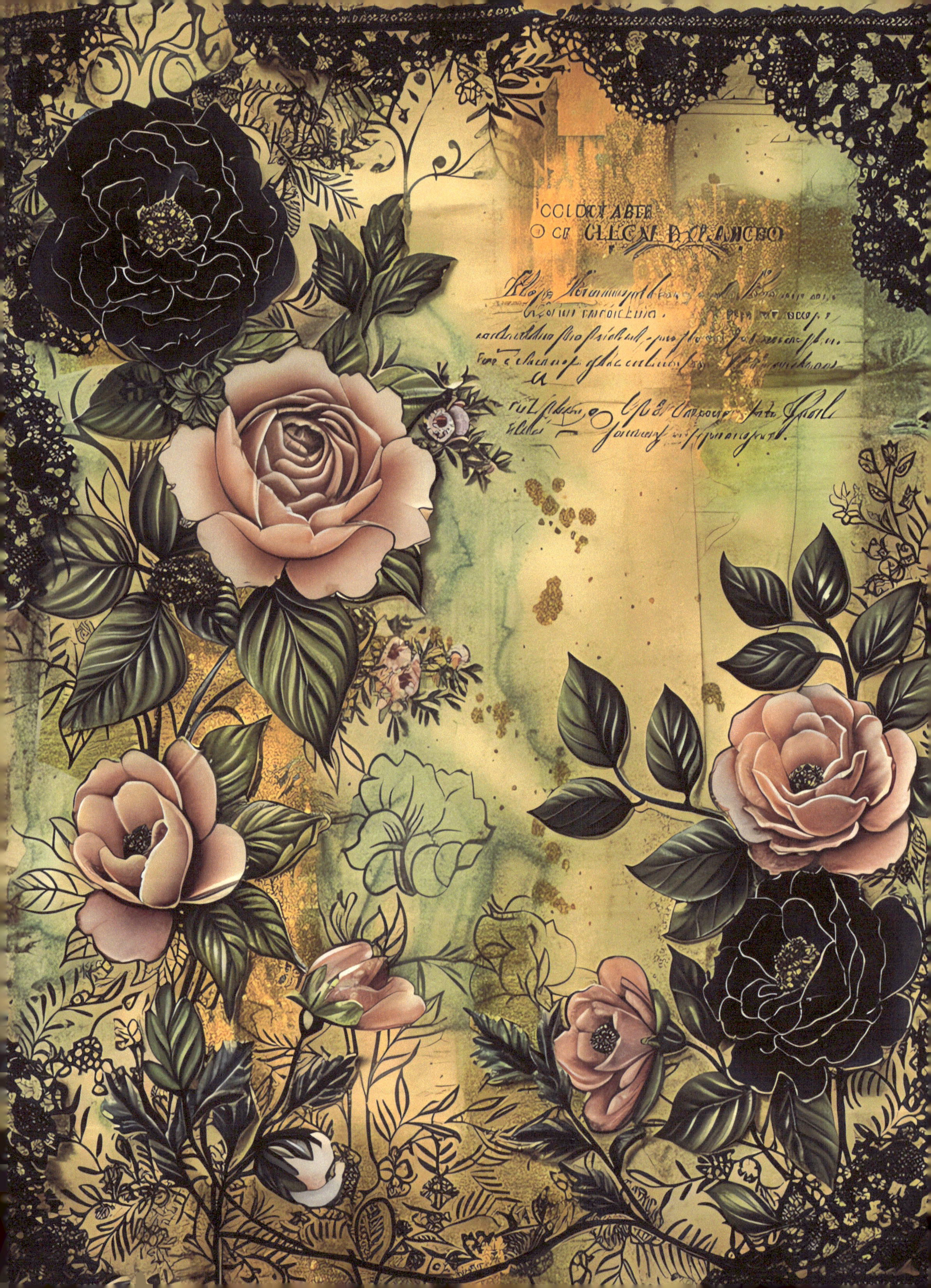

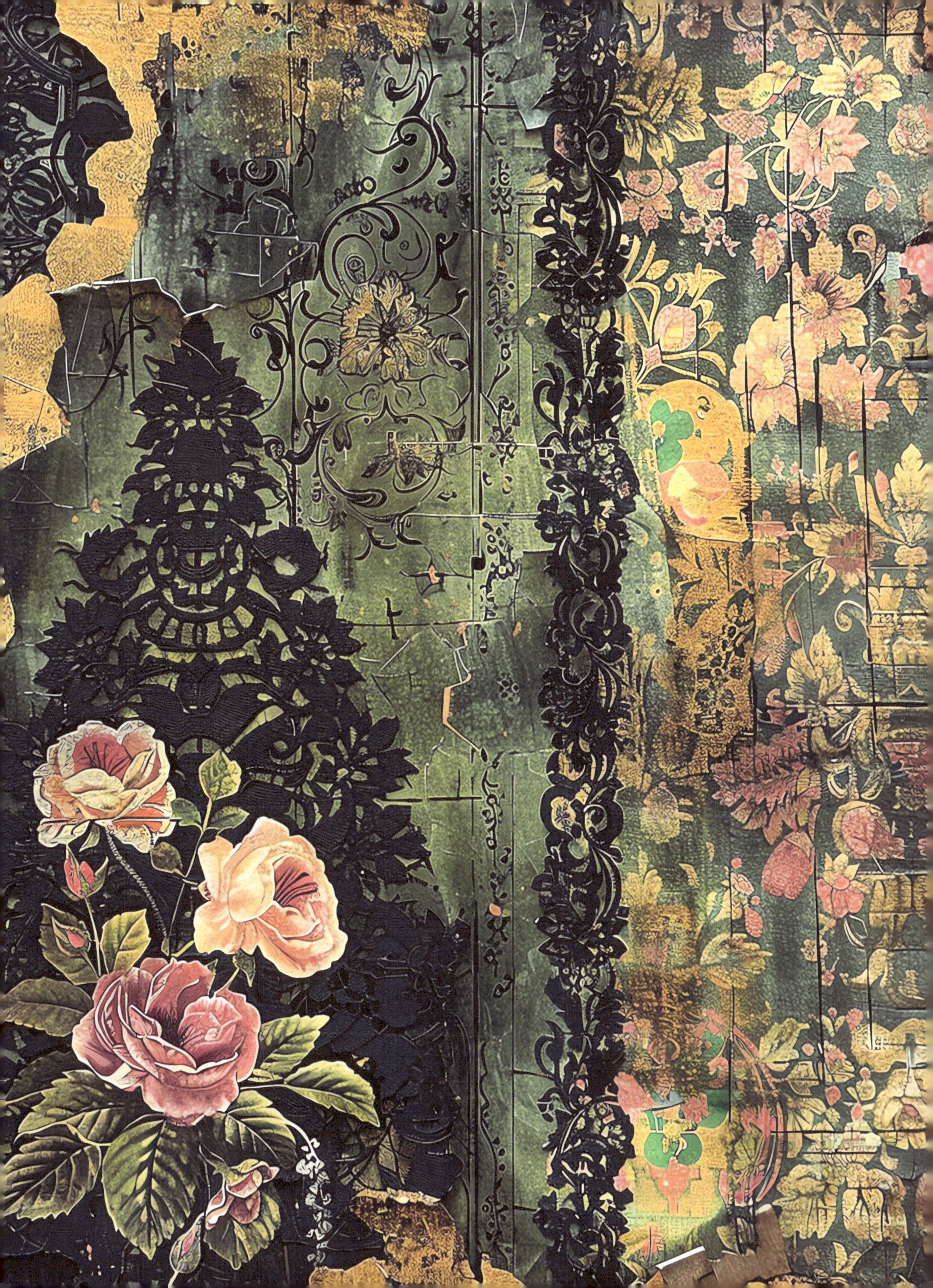

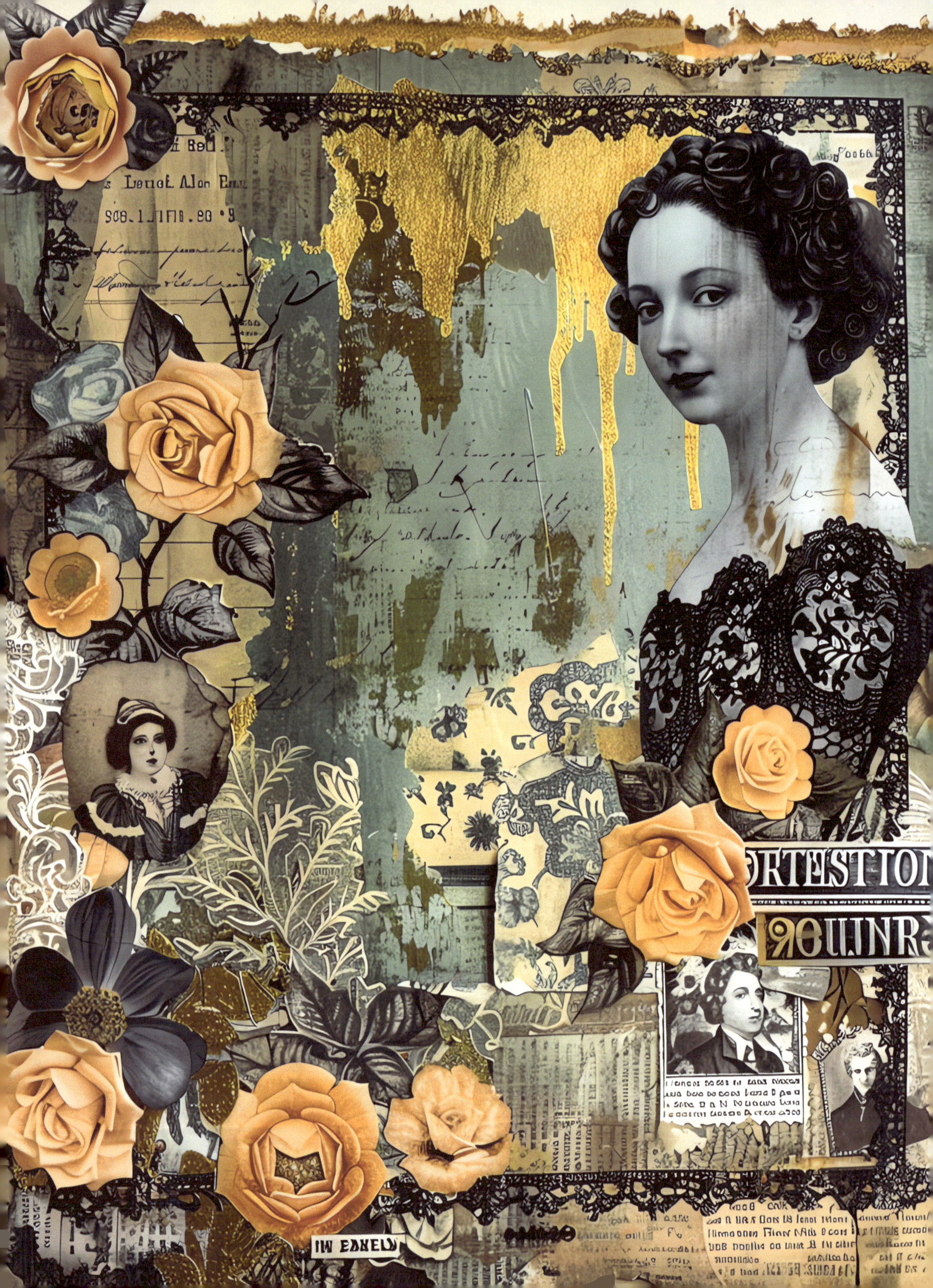
ORTESTION
IW EANELY

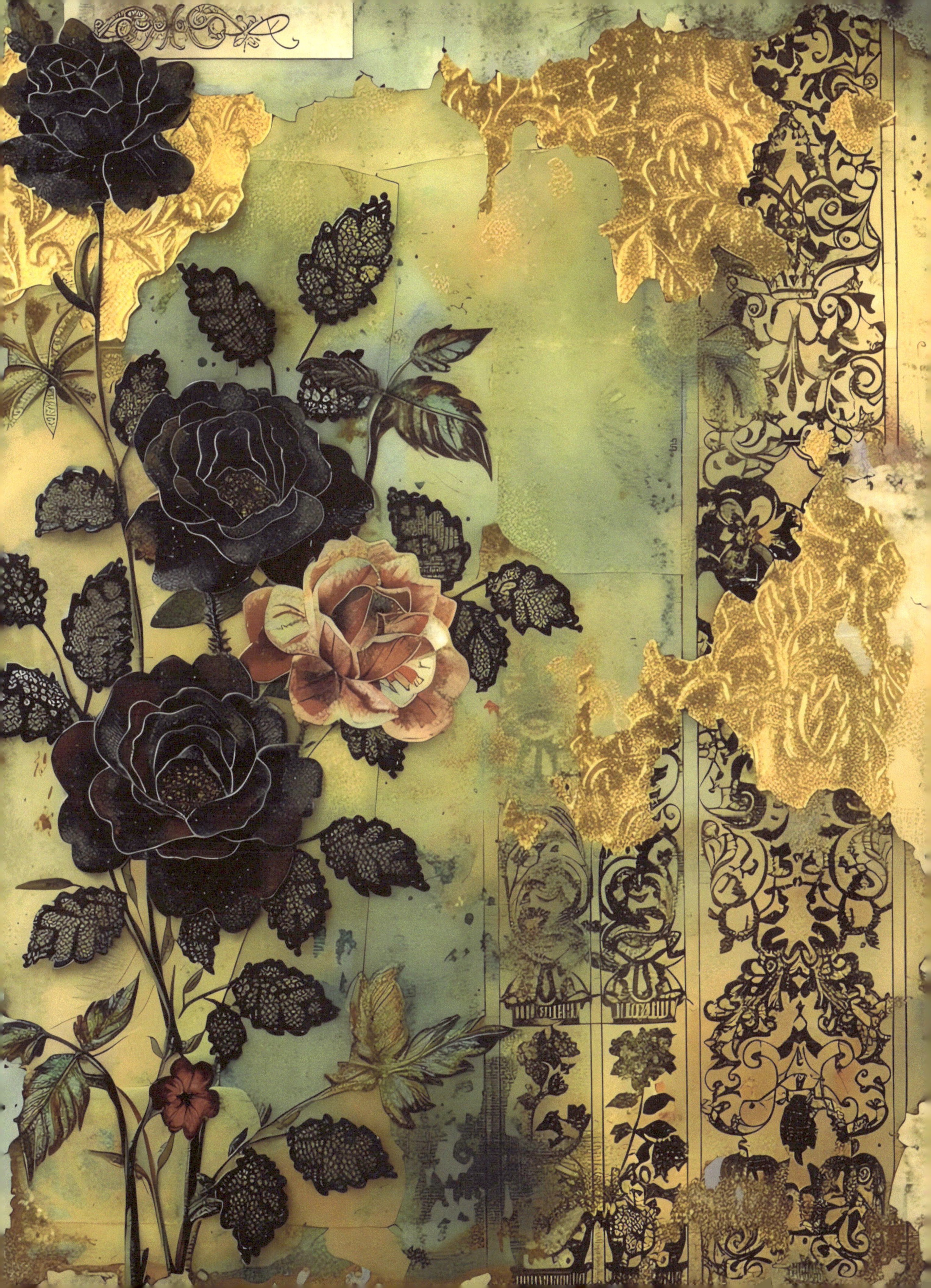

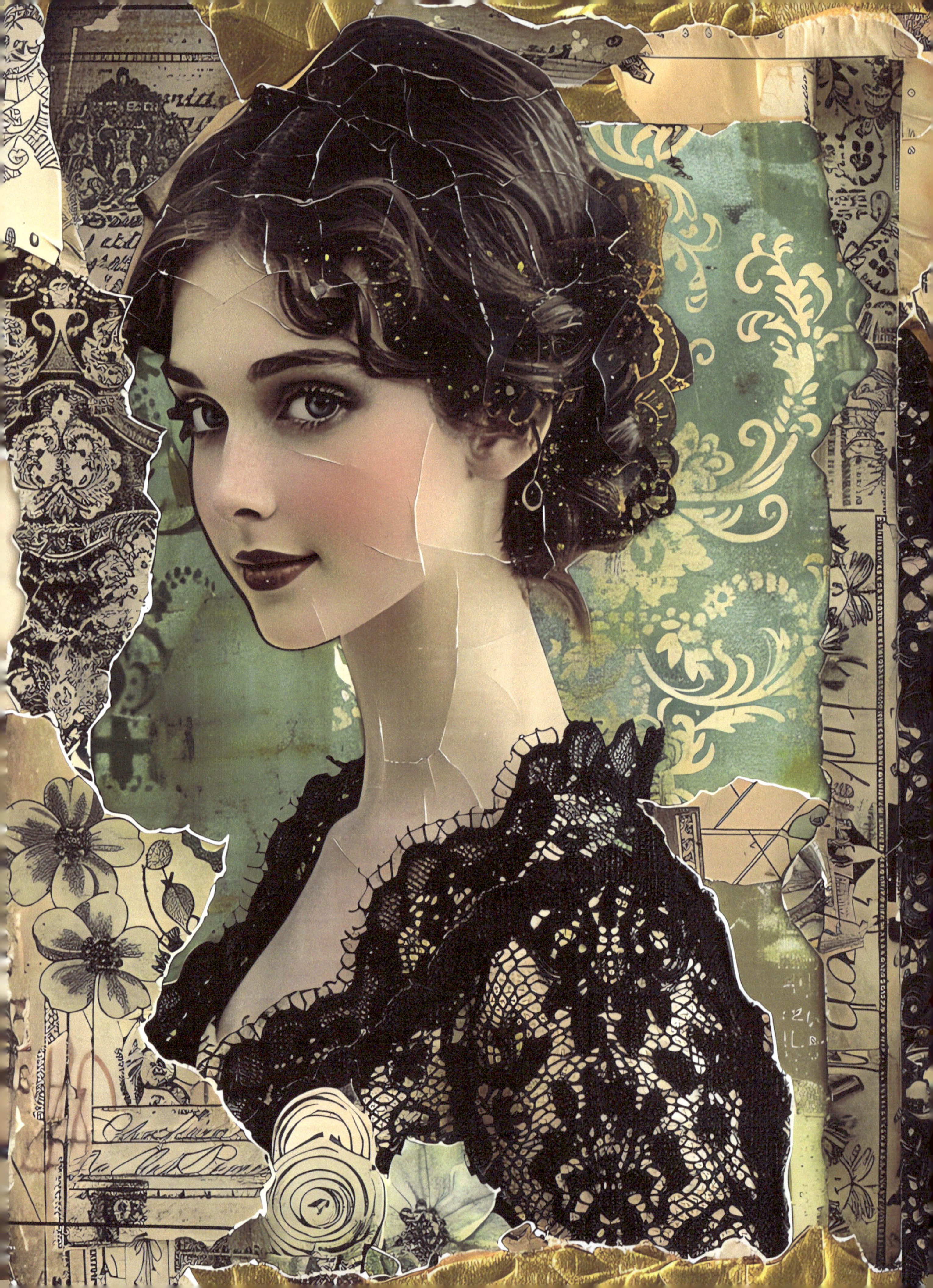

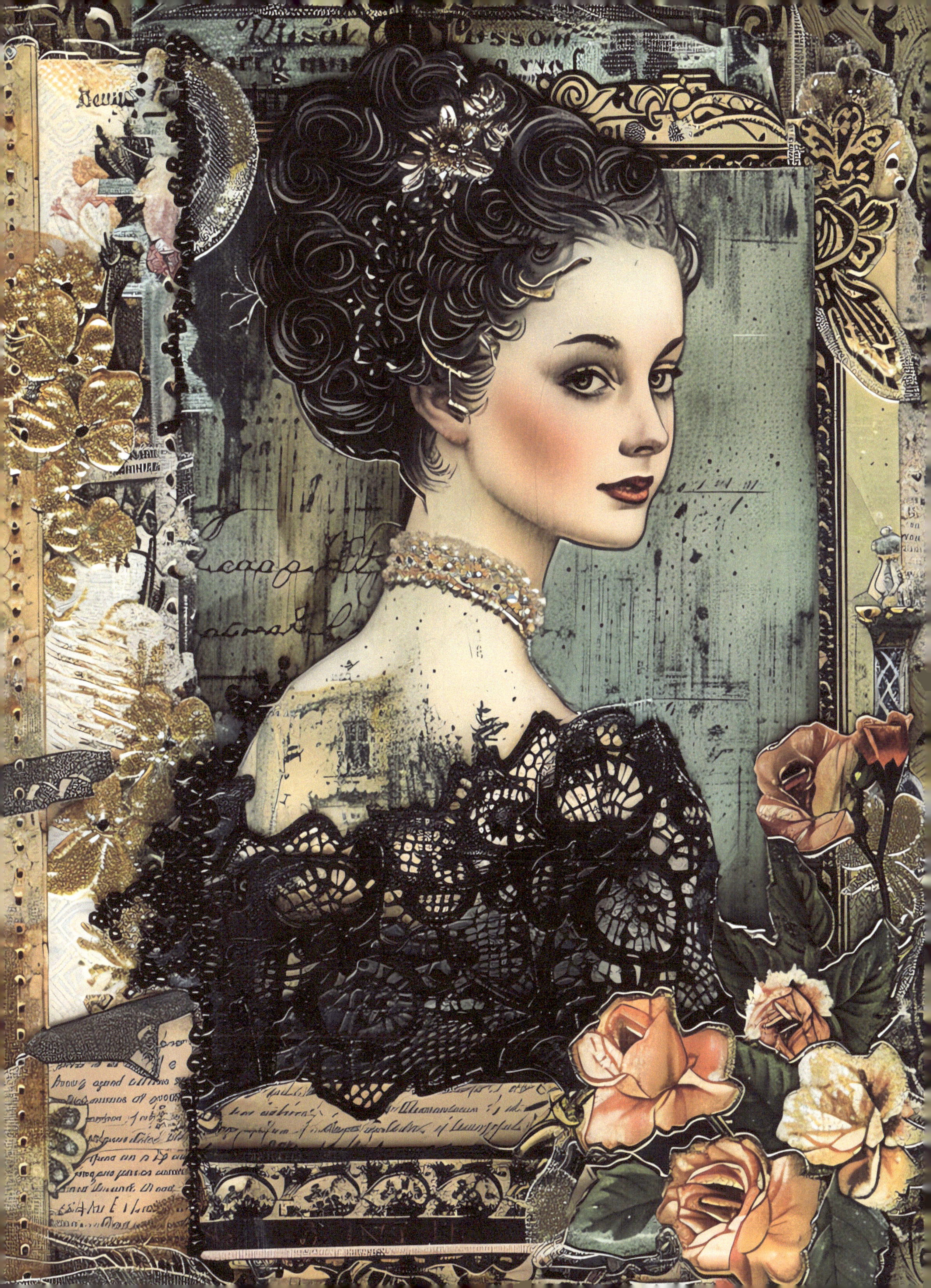

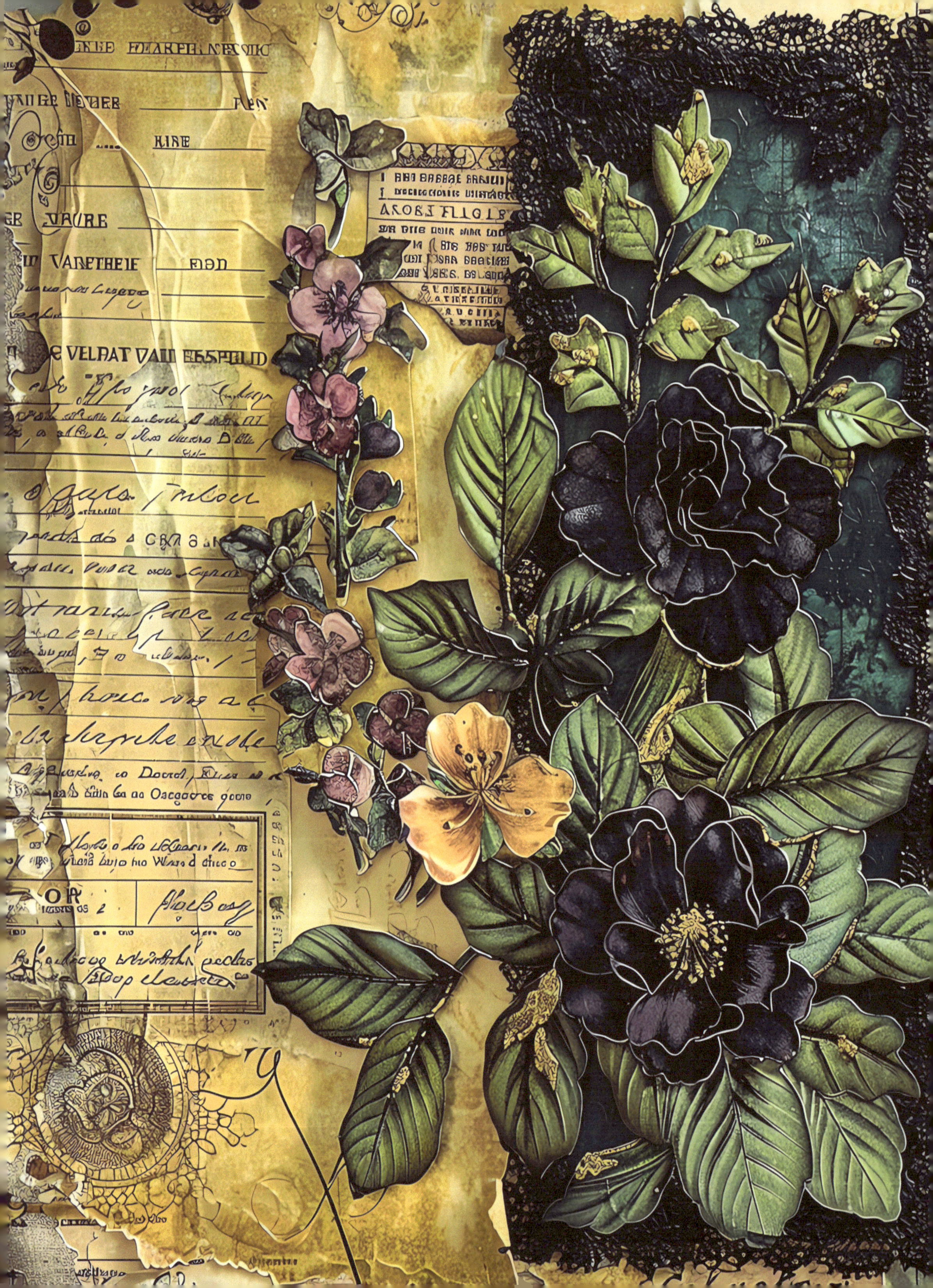

www.ingramcontent.com/pod-product-compliance
Lightning Source LLC
Chambersburg PA
CBHW040448220526
45473CB00004B/1563
9798301327636